BECAUSE I AM A GIRL

Proceeds from sales of this book go to Plan, one of the world's largest and oldest child-centred community development organisations. Plan works in 66 countries on programmes and initiatives that address the causes of poverty and its consequences for children's rights and their lives. They work locally, embedded in a community, to educate, encourage and build the skills and resources necessary to create positive changes in the lives of children and their families.

TIM BUTCHER, XIAOLU GUO,
JOANNE HARRIS, KATHY LETTE,
DEBORAH MOGGACH, MARIE PHILLIPS,
SUBHADRA BELBASE AND IRVINE WELSH

Because I am a Girl

VINTAGE BOOKS
London

First published by Vintage 2010

2 4 6 8 10 9 7 5 3 1

Vintage
Random House, 20 Vauxhall Bridge Road,
London SW1V 2SA

www.vintage-books.co.uk

Addresses for companies within The Random House Group Limited
can be found at: www.randomhouse.co.uk/offices.htm

The Random House Group Limited Reg. No. 954009

A CIP catalogue record for this book
is available from the British Library

ISBN 9780099535928

The Random House Group Limited supports The Forest
Stewardship Council (FSC), the leading international forest
certification organisation. All our titles that are printed on
Greenpeace approved FSC certified paper carry the FSC logo.
Our paper procurement policy can be found at:
www.rbooks.co.uk/environment

Printed and bound in Great Britain by
CPI Bookmarque, Croydon CR0 4TD

Contents

Foreword

MARIE STAUNTON, CHIEF
EXECUTIVE OF PLAN UK

'How do you feel sending these girls out into the street every night, knowing what will happen to them?' I asked. A pretty stupid question, as my fifteen-year-old daughter commented later. I was visiting a hostel in Alexandria where, during the day, teachers and counsellors supported homeless girls. But while the boys' hostel is open day and night, the Egyptian authorities do not allow overnight stays in the girls' hostel. So, at five o'clock every afternoon, girls as young as nine are given a little bag with soap and a first-aid kit, and locked out of the only home they know. In years of working all over the world nothing has affected me quite like that image so, yes, perhaps it was a stupid question.

To survive on the streets, these girls have to join one of the hundreds of gangs in Alexandria, whose joining fee is sexual abuse by older gang members. The authorities believe that girls who are not virgins, who are now 'ladies' are automatically the responsibility of their non-existent husbands. And this blind presumption means that the girls are officially invisible, leaving them, often with their own babies, at the mercy of all the predators on the street.

This book was compiled to make such girls visible in a way that reports and statistics cannot. Recently Plan published research which showed that in many countries girls as young as ten have sex with their teachers to secure better grades. The research received no coverage in the UK's media.

How to make these victims visible? I remember travelling to a forgotten famine in remotest Sudan with the journalist Bill Deedes. His subsequent report – a simple story powerfully told – shocked readers and prodded governments into action. I enrolled the help of publishers The Random House Group in order to find writers who were willing to go to the places where girls get a raw deal – where girls are fed less than their brothers; are more likely to be taken out of school; are more likely to be abused – and tell their stories.

Writers see with a different eye than development workers. Some responded with passion. Marie Phillips was appalled that the responsibility for sexual abuse was placed on Ugandan schoolgirls, not their abusers.

Kathy Lette was no less passionate but used her wit to illuminate the lives of girls in Brazil in a hilarious but biting story.

Joanne Harris established a strong rapport with the girls she met. Perhaps because of her career in teaching she has an ability to get alongside young people. She shadowed a day in the life of a young girl named Kadeka. As I was sitting in the middle of a village in Togo peeling pimentos, I heard gusts of laughter followed by the appearance of Joanne bent double under a huge load of firewood, the same amount that Kadeka was carrying with apparent ease.

In contrast, Irvine Welsh avoided engagement during his visit to the Dominican Republic. He sidestepped formal meetings, watched from the outside and asked simple, practical questions: the name of a tree, the meaning of a word. His story was a total surprise, but it met with instant recognition from Plan workers in the Dominican Republic – yes, they said, that's it. He has got what happens here. How did he do that?

Deborah Moggach is a listener. The story she wrote may be fiction but weaves together the many true stories that she drew out of the girls she met. Sitting under her big hat in the shade, gently questioning them with patience and with charm.

Xiaolu Guo is a filmmaker as well as a writer. She also resisted formal engagement and information that came from any sort of official voice. She watched and filmed and found out about the history of the country and its people. She internalised an atmosphere, and her story is true to that.

Tim Butcher approached the assignment as a journalist. Travelling in Liberia and Sierra Leone in the footsteps of Graham Greene, he interviewed girls damaged by war and produced a piece of fiction reflecting the fact that they were still being damaged by peace

As the authors wrote up their stories, the lives of many girls they had met were rocked by the global financial crisis. The annual report that Plan compiles, *The State of the World's Girls*, showed that in 2009 the financial upheaval took a heavy toll on families and communities everywhere, and that when money is short it is girls and women who are the most affected. The World Bank estimates that in 2009 alone an additional 50,000 African children will die before their first birthday, and most of those will be girls. The Bank's Managing Director, Ngozi Okonjo-Iweala, wrote in her introduction to the 2009 report:

> As a young girl growing up in Nigeria poverty is never a theory. Living on under $1.25 a day was a reality . . . and I clearly remember when I had to carry my younger sister on my back and walk for five miles to save her life from malaria. Looking

back it was education and a caring and supportive family that opened the door to success for me . . . Investing in girls is an efficient way of breaking intergenerational cycles of poverty. Educated girls become educated mothers with increased livelihood prospects; they also have a greater propensity than similarly educated males to invest in children's schooling.

Seventy years of experience, working with nine million children across the world, has shown the charity I am part of, Plan, that investing in girls is crucial to breaking the cycle of poverty. We are launching the Because I am a Girl (BIG) campaign to break the cycle of uneducated mothers giving birth much too young to underweight babies who in turn grow up to be unhealthy and uneducated. As part of the campaign, we are following a group of little girls and their families until 2015. One of those girls is Brenda, whose mother Adina was only thirteen when she gave birth to Brenda, her second child. Brenda is now three, and already it is clear that her young mother is struggling to nurture her family. Brenda is withdrawn and often hungry; she is already at a disadvantage and will find it hard to do well at school, if she gets there in the first place.

The twentieth century is considered by most in the developed world to have brought massive progress in female emancipation, and discrimination against girls in education is rarely a major issue, although many may hit their heads against a glass ceiling once they leave school. But poorer parts of the world have not seen even this amount of progress. Today's girls face new threats – urbanisation means more girls, like those in Alexandria, are living unprotected on the streets; during modern conflicts in countries like Liberia, rape is used as a weapon of war.

President Ellen Johnson Sirleaf, the first female Head of State of Liberia, wrote in the 2008 *State of the World's Girls* report:

> Fifty per cent of (Liberia's) population is under eighteen years old and girls make up more than half of this group. Liberian girls experience gender-based violence by older men in their neighbourhoods and by their teachers on a daily basis . . . I believe that securing the future for our girls is critical to achieving national development. The popular saying 'when you educate a man you feed his family but when you educate a woman, you educate a nation' is profound.

Graca Machel, in her support for our annual report, *The State of the World's Girls*, said, 'We can no longer accept that girls should not be valued simply because they are not boys.' Girls around the world have been told by so many people for such a long time that they are worthless, so of course they start to believe this. The BIG campaign aims to reverse the lack of belief and investment in girls. Join us by clicking on www.becauseiamagirl.org

Thank you to all the writers in this book for enduring tough travel schedules and difficult living-conditions to produce unique and enthralling writing, and to Rachel Cugnoni and Frances Macmillan at Vintage Books for their inspiration and understanding. It is only right to give the last word to a girl:

Someday I will prove that I am no less than my brothers
Rakhi, 17

Marie Staunton, Chief Executive of Plan UK, 2009

Road Song

JOANNE HARRIS

Joanne Harris is the author of the Whitbread-shortlisted *Chocolat* (made into a major film starring Juliette Binoche), *Blackberry Wine*, *Five Quarters of the Orange*, *Coastliners*, *Holy Fools*, *Jigs & Reels*, *Sleep Pale Sister*, *Gentlemen & Players*, *The Lollipop Shoes* and, with Fran Warde, *The French Kitchen: A Cookbook* and *The French Market: More Recipes from a French Kitchen*. She lives in Huddersfield, Yorkshire, with her husband and daughter.

There are so many gods here. Rain gods; death gods; river gods; wind gods. Gods of the maize; medicine gods; old gods; new gods brought here from elsewhere and gone native, sinking their roots into the ground, sending out signals and stories and songs wherever the wind will take them.

Such a god is the Great North Road. From Lomé by the Bight of Benin to Dapaong in the far provinces, it runs like a dusty river. Its source, the city of Lomé, with its hot and humid streets; its markets; its gracious boulevards; its beach and the litter of human jetsam that roams along the esplanade, and the shoals of mopeds and bicycles that make up most of its traffic. Unlike the river, even in drought the Great North Road never runs dry. Nor does its burden of legends and songs; of travellers and their stories.

My tale begins right here, outside the town of Sokodé. A large and busy settlement five hours' drive north of Lomé, ringed with smaller villages like handmaids to the greater town. All depend on the road for their existence, although many of these villagers have never been very much further than a few dozen miles to the north or south. Often people walk up the track and sit and watch and wait by the side of the road for whatever flotsam it may bring; traders on cycles; mopeds; trucks; women on their way to the fields to harvest maize or to cut wood.

One of these watchers is Adjo, a girl from nearby Kassena. Sixteen years old; the eldest of five; she likes to sit in the shade of the trees as the road unwinds before her. Her younger brother Marcellin used to watch the sky for vapour-trails, while Jean-Baptiste preferred the trucks, waving madly as they passed, but Adjo just watches the road, ever alert for a sign of life. Over the years she has come to believe that the road is more than just dirt and stones; it has a force, an identity. She also believes that it has a *voice* – sometimes just a distant hiss, sometimes many voices, compelling as a church choir.

And in the mornings at five o'clock, when she gets up to begin her chores, the road is already waiting for her; humming faintly; sheathed in mist. It might almost be asleep; but Adjo knows better. The road is like a crocodile; one eye open even in sleep, ready to snap at anyone foolish enough to drop their guard. Adjo never drops her guard. As she ties her sarong into place; knots it firmly at her hip; ties the *bandeau* across her breasts; slips barefoot across the yard; draws water from the village well; hauls it back to the washing hut; as she cuts the firewood and ties it into a bundle, as she carries it home on her head, she listens for the song of the road; she watches its sly, insidious length and the dust that rises with the sun, announcing the presence of visitors.

This morning, the road is almost silent. A few bats circle above a stand of banyan trees; a woman with a bundle of sticks crosses from the other side; something small – a bush-rat, perhaps – rattles through the undergrowth. If they were here, Adjo thinks, her brothers would go out hunting today. They would set fire to the dry brush downwind of the village, and wait for the bush-rats to come running out of the burning grass. There's plenty of meat on a bush-rat – it's tougher than chicken, but tasty – and then they would sell them by the road, gutted and stretched on a framework of sticks, to folk on their way to the market.

But Adjo's brothers are long gone, like many of the children. No-one will hunt bush-rat today, or stand by the road at Sokodé, waving at the vehicles. No-one will play *ampé* with her in the yard, or lie on their backs under the trees watching out for vapour-trails.

She drops the cut wood to the ground outside the open kitchen door. Adjo's home is a compound of mud-brick buildings with a corrugated iron roof around a central yard area. There is a henhouse, a maize store, a row of low benches on which to sit and a cooking pot at the far end. Adjo's mother uses this pot to brew *tchoukoutou*, millet beer, which she sells around the village, or to make soy cheese or maize porridge for sale at the weekly market in Sokodé.

Adjo likes the market. There are so many things to see there. Young men riding mopeds; women riding pillion. Sellers of manioc and fried plantain. Flatbed trucks bearing timber. *Vaudou* men selling spells and charms. Dough-ball stands by the roadside. Pancakes and *foufou*; yams and bananas; mountains of millet and peppers and rice. Fabrics of all colours; sarongs and scarves and *dupattas*. Bead necklaces, bronze earrings; tins of *harissa*; bangles; pottery dishes; bottles and gourds; spices and salt; garlands of chillies; cooking pots; brooms; baskets; plastic buckets; knives; Coca-Cola; engine oil and sandals made from plaited grass.

Most of these things are beyond the means of Adjo and her family. But she likes to watch as she helps her mother prepare maize porridge for sale at their stall, grinding the meal between two stones, then cooking it in a deep pan. And the song of the road is more powerful here; a song of distant places; of traders and travellers, gossip and news, of places whose names she knows only from maps chalked on to a blackboard.

The road has seen Adjo travel to and from markets every day since she could walk. Sometimes she makes her way alone; most often she walks with her mother, balancing the maize on her head in a woven basket. Until two years ago, she went to school, and the road saw her walk the other way, dressed in a white blouse and khaki skirt and carrying a parcel of books. In those days its song was different; it sang of mathematics and English and geography; of dictionaries and football matches and music and hope. But since her brothers left home, Adjo no longer walks to school, or wears the khaki uniform. And the song of the road has changed again; now it sings of marriage, and home; and children running in the yard; and of long days spent in the maize fields, and of childish dreams put away for good.

It isn't as if she *wanted* to leave. She was a promising student. Almost as clever as a boy, and almost as good at football, too – even the Chief has commented, though grudgingly (he does not approve of girls' football). But with a husband away all year round, and younger children to care for – all three with malaria, and one not even two years old – Adjo's mother needs help, and although she feels sad for her daughter, she knows that reading-books never fed anyone, or ploughed as much as a square inch of land.

Besides, she thinks, when the boys come home there will be money for everyone; money for clothes, for medicine, for food – in Nigeria, she has heard, people eat chicken every day, and everyone has a radio, a mosquito net, a sewing machine.

This is the song the mother hears. A lullaby of dreams come true, and it sounds to her like Adjale's voice – Adjale, of the golden smile – and although she misses her boys, she knows that one day they will both come home, bringing the wealth she was promised. It's hard to send her children away – two young boys, barely into their teens – into a foreign city. But sacrifices must be made, so Adjale has told her. And they will be cared for very well. Each boy will have a bicycle; each boy will have a mobile phone. Such riches seem impossible here in Togo; but in Nigeria, things are different. The houses have tiled floors; a bath; water; electricity. Employers are kind and respectful; they care for the children as if they were their own. Even the girls are given new clothes, jewellery and make-up. Adjale told her all this – Adjale, with the golden voice – when the traffickers first came.

Traffickers. Such a cruel word. Adjo's mother prefers to call them *fishers of men*, like Jesus and his disciples. Their river is the Great North Road; and every year, they travel north like fishermen to the spawning grounds. Every year they come away with a plentiful catch of boys and girls, many as young as twelve or thirteen, like Marcellin and Jean-Baptiste. They smuggle them over the border by night, avoiding the police patrols, for none of them have a passport. Sometimes they take them over the river on rafts made of wood and plastic drums, lashed together with twine woven from the banana leaf.

Road Song

Adjo's mother wonders if, on the day her sons return, she will even recognise them. Both will have grown into men by now. Her heart swells painfully at the thought. And she thinks of her daughter, Adjo – so clever, so young, with red string woven into her hair and the voice of an angel – still waiting, after all this time. And when the daily chores are done, and the red sun fades from the western sky, and the younger children are asleep on their double pallet in the hut, she watches Adjo as she stands perfectly still by the Great North Road, etched in the light of the village fires, singing softly to herself and praying for her brothers' return.

For Adjo knows that the road is a god, a dangerous god that must be appeased. Sometimes it takes a stray child, or maybe, if they are lucky, a dog – crushed beneath some lorry's wheels. But the traffickers take more than that; four children last year; three gone the year before. So Adjo sings; *Don't let them come; please, this year, keep them away* – and she is not entirely sure whether it is to God or Allah that she prays or to the Great North Road itself, the sly and dusty snake-god that charms away their children.

By night the road seems more than ever alive; filled with rumours and whisperings. All the old, familiar sounds from the village down the path – the chanting, the drumming, the children at play, the warble of a radio or a mobile phone from outside the Chief's house, where the men drink *tchouk* and talk business – now all these things seem so far away, as distant as the aeroplanes that some-times track their paths overhead, leaving those broken vapour-trails like fingernail-scratches across the sky. Only the road is real, she thinks; the road with its songs of seduction, to which we sacrifice our children for the sake of a beautiful lie, a shining dream of better things.

She knows that most will never come back. She needs no songs to tell her *that*. The fishers of men are predators, with their shining lure of salvation. The truth is they come like the harmattan, the acrid wind that blows every year, stripping the land of its moisture and filling the mouth with a sour red dust. Nothing grows while the harmattan blows, except for the dreams of foolish boys and their even more foolish mothers, who send them off with the traffickers – all dressed in their church clothes, in case the patrols spot them and smell their desperation – each with a thick slice of cold maize porridge, lovingly wrapped up in a fold of banana leaf and tied with a piece of red string, for luck.

Money changes hands – not much, not even the price of a sackful of grain, but the baby needs a mosquito net, and the older one some medicine, and she isn't *selling* her children, Adjo's mother tells herself; she is sending them to the Promised Land. Adjale will look after them. Adjale, who every year brings news of her sons and tells her: *maybe next year they will send a card, a letter, even a photograph –*

But something inside her still protests, and once again

she asks herself whether she did the right thing. And every year Adjale smiles and says to her; *Trust me. I know what I'm doing.* And though it's very hard for her to see him only once a year, she knows that he is doing well, helping children along the road, and he has promised to send for her — *one day, very soon,* he says. *Just as soon as the children are grown. Four years, maybe five, that's all.*

And Adjo's mother believes him. He *has* been very good to her. But Adjo does not trust him. She has never trusted him. But what can one girl do alone? She cannot stop them any more than she could stop the harmattan with its yearly harvest of red dust. *What can I do?* she asks the road. *What can I do to fight them?*

The answer comes to her that night, as she stands alone by the side of the road. The moon is high in the sky, and yet, the road is still warm, like an animal; and it smells of dust and petrol, and of the sweat of the many bare feet that pound its surface daily. And maybe the road answers her prayer, or maybe another god is listening; but tonight, only to Adjo — it tells another story; it sings a song of loneliness; of sadness and betrayal. It sings of sick children left to die along the road to Nigeria; of girls sold into prostitution; of thwarted hopes and violence and sickness and starvation and AIDS. It sings of disappointment; and of two boys with the scars of Kassena cut into their cheeks, their bodies covered in sour red dust, coming home up the Great North Road. The boys are penniless, starving and sick after two long years in Nigeria, working the fields fourteen hours a day, sold for the price of a bicycle. *But still alive*, Adjo thinks; *still alive and coming home*; and the pounding beat of this new song joins the beat of Adjo's heart as she stands by the road at Kassena, and her feet begin to move in the dust; and her body begins to lilt and sway; and in that moment she hears them all; all those vanished children; all of them joining the voice of the road in a song that will not be ignored.

And now she understands what to do to fight the fishers of children. It isn't much, but it *is* a start; it's the seed that grows into a tree; the tree that becomes a forest; the forest that forms a windbreak that may even stop the harmattan.

Not today. Not this year. But maybe in her lifetime –

Now *that* would be a thing to see.

Walking home that night past the fires; as Adjo walks past the Chief's hut; past the maize field; past the rows of pot-bellied henhouses; as she washes her face at the water-pump; as she drinks from a hollowed-out gourd and eats the slice of cold maize porridge her mother has left on the table for her; as she lays out her old school uniform, the white blouse and khaki skirt and the battered old football boots that she has not yet outgrown; as she lies down on her mattress and listens to the sounds of the night, Adjo thinks about *other* roads; the paths we have to make for ourselves.

Tomorrow, she thinks, will be different. Tomorrow,

instead of watching the road, instead of going to market, she will walk up to the schoolhouse wearing her khaki uniform; swinging her boots by the laces in time to the song only she can hear. Her mother will try to stop her, perhaps; but only with a half of her heart. And when her brothers come home at last, she will tell them: *Why did you leave? The Promised Land was always here. Inside me. Inside you.* And maybe, in time, she will make them hear this song she hears so clearly; and maybe their children will hear it too, and understand her when she says: *If the road doesn't take you where you want, then you must make your own road.*

There are so many gods here in this land of Togo. River gods; road gods; all of them, maybe, false gods. But the real power lies in the human heart; its courage; its resilience. This, too, is the song of the road, and through the voices of children it endures, and grows more powerful every day; sinking its roots deep into the soil, sending out its seeds of change wherever the wind will take them.

Bendu's Dream

TIM BUTCHER

Tim Butcher is an award-winning journalist, broadcaster and bestselling author. His first book, *Blood River: A Journey to Africa's Broken Heart*, recounting an epic journey he made through the Congo in the footsteps of Henry Morton Stanley, was published in 2007 and shortlisted for the Samuel Johnson Prize for Non-Fiction. Formerly a foreign correspondent for the *Daily Telegraph*, he divides his time between London and Cape Town.

The dream was so vivid it woke Bendu and for a few seconds, as she lay blinking on her grass mattress getting her bearings, strands of recall flickered at the edge of her mind. There are some dreams, she told herself, that are meant to be remembered and this was one of them. Knowing how after looking directly at the sun you can close your eyes and still see its glare, she screwed her eyes tight shut. Slowly the dream came back to her.

The first thing she remembered was the noise. There was an inhuman howling accompanied by rustling and scuffling but she had difficulty making out where it came from. The scene was lit by a strange half-light, a bit like when the harmattan wind blows, clogging the skies over West Africa with dust from the Sahara, but she could clearly see a group of other teenage girls. They were moaning with fear.

She could not quite recognise their faces but they were composites of individuals with whom she had shared episodes of her troubled life – a hairstyle from a classmate she was held hostage with, a cotton lappa wrap with a distinctive curly seashell design. The last time she saw that lappa it was being used as a shroud by a young mother, hollow with grief for an infant who died of starvation while fleeing through the bush.

In her dream she turned round slowly to see what was causing the others so much terror.

Cloaked in raffia and capped by a headpiece carved from black wood, showing a snouted creature's face with tusks and wide eyes, it was impossible to tell quite how large the being was. One moment it crouched motionless, low to the ground, the mask no higher than waist height and the grass tresses of its coat hanging limply, and then, with an explosion of dust and screeching, it span and shook, the mask now towering high above Bendu's head, the raffia startled with energy.

The dance stoked pure fear among the others but the thing that made the dream so memorable for Bendu, the thing that made her screw shut her eyes extra tight to check she was remembering correctly, was how she had reacted. Instead of reeling away, Bendu recalled how at ease she felt as she broke away from her cowering companions and walked forward, her hands outstretched in welcome.

At this the creature seemed to become even wilder. Its cries became more demented, the dust thrown up by its gyrations grew thicker and the carved wooden mask loomed ever higher throbbing with more menace. And that is when the dream ended.

*

Bendu blinked her eyes shut a few more times but the image had gone. In its place were the shapes, smells and sounds of her small rented room in a mud-walled hut and her life far up country in Sierra Leone, or 'up-line' as she was taught to say, in an echo of colonial days when a railway line, long defunct, connected the capital, Freetown, with the provinces.

She was about as far from Freetown as it was possible to be inside Sierra Leone, in what had once been a busy trading town called Kailahun. Its position close to the country's far eastern border with neighbouring Guinea and Liberia had, in its day, been a blessing, ensuring cross-border trade and a sense of open horizons as outsiders journeyed through with their different languages, customs and ideas. There had been Mandingo traders, the wanderers of West Africa who stood out with the flowing gowns and brightly coloured fezzes. Their Islamic faith and desire for profit cared little for international boundaries. And there were ambitious Krio administrators from Freetown who came out to the provinces with their textbooks and college degrees determined to drag rural Africa into the modern world. And there were even a few white missionaries, remnants of an earlier age when seeding Christianity in the heathen hinterland of Africa was seen as the way forward for a continent.

But in recent years those horizons had closed in on

Kailahun and its location had been its curse. When Liberian warlords set about stirring conflict in Sierra Leone it was through Kailahun that their rebels and guns flooded. As more and more of Sierra Leone fell to the gunmen, so Kailahun became a transit point for gems flowing out of the country's diamond fields and blood money flowing in. A once major town was destroyed and though the war had officially ended years before there remained in Kailahun a very immediate post-tsunami air, a strong and still current sense of shock at the scale and cruelty of the battering it had endured.

Bendu's life had spanned those awful times although she remembered little of what she had actually witnessed. She knew her parents were both dead, killed in the first attack on the village where she was born just outside Kailahun. The story went that she had been found still bound by a lappa to her dead mother's back and taken in by one of the rebel army's female camp followers. That woman had in turn been killed in a later counter-attack and Bendu had spent the next years as flotsam on the war's ebb and flow.

Forced to work as a slave for various armed factions, she spent years on the move, making temporary home in the ruins of war-damaged villages or out in the forest. There were moments when she had been forced to carry a gun, shooting madly into the forest in what was later described with pride, though scant honesty, as 'military operations'. There had been assaults by men if that's the right word for the armed brutes often not much older than her. She could remember the rancid smell of palm wine on their breath and the glazed unseeing eyes as they crushed the last remnants of her childhood out of her.

Since the war ended, child psychologists sent by aid groups had come to treat her almost as a special case. War crimes investigators had endured the eighteen-hour drive all the way across Sierra Leone to speak to her. Apparently one of the rebels she had spent time serving, Issay, was a 'kakatua', the so-called Big Fish responsible for the worst atrocities of the war and the investigators came with their notebooks and tape recorders to take down what Bendu remembered.

But she had deliberately kept the details from lodging permanently in her mind. Her past was too distressing. Like many in Sierra Leone she saw no point in looking backwards and trying to pin blame. There were too many in the community who had taken part in atrocities that to hold them all to account would eat out society and leave nothing in its place. But she remembered how Issay justified everything – child soldiers, rapes, killing – with the same remark: 'In Africa your elders know best.'

After the operation she underwent at the United Nations hospital when she was told she would never be able to have children, she made herself try to look forwards, to think of tomorrow, not yesterday. All that mattered now was earning enough from growing and selling rice to pay the rent on her room in Kailahun, and keeping her place at Methodist Girls' High – MGH – the oldest school in the region and the first to reopen after the war.

She struggled to sleep again after the dream but dawn was still some way off. Murky moonlight came through her un-curtained window allowing her to make out the outline of her possessions. There was the rattan armchair, fashioned by her landlord and paid for by a month of skivvying – slavery, most would call it – for his spiteful wife. Bendu half-smiled at the memory of a month being chided by that woman. 'Switch bitch' she called her because of the rattan switch she carried and the willingness with which she used it. The silly woman thought she was all-powerful with her cane but Bendu never let her win. What Bendu had gone through during the war, the suffering and pain she had endured, meant she could easily take a beating. The woman screeched at Bendu to do as she was told, using the words the warlord Issay had used – 'In Africa your elders know best.'

On the chair lay Bendu's entire wardrobe: a few changes of clothes, cleaned, pressed, folded and capped by the felt school hat required by MGH. And on the wall were the two possessions she loved most. From one of the bare pole rafters hung a poster showing a football player from a team called Arsenal. She did not know where the man came from or what the name, Arsenal, might represent, but the fact he was black, successful and oh-so handsome gave it a special place in her heart.

And next to the poster on the same wall, hanging from a twig stuck into the mud, was her favourite object – a small, plastic-framed mirror. For most of her life Bendu had not known what she looked like – buying that looking-glass a year or so after the war ended from a Mandingo trader, one of the first to return to Kailahun after the fighting, had felt like the moment when her life had begun again.

The room was silent except for the flurrying of rats in the dried banana leaf thatch but she could tell by the smell of charcoal smoke that the day would be starting soon. It meant Ma Fata, the old lady who lived in the hut the other side of the clearing, was awake and preparing for another day.

The smell gave Bendu an idea. 'Ma Fata is old and knows a lot. She will know the meaning of my dream.' The thought gave her the energy she needed to get out of bed, wrap herself in her lappa and take the mile-long round trip to the stream so she could fill her plastic water basin. By the time she began the slow walk back to her hut, with the full basin settled heavily on her head, the cocks had begun to crow.

*

As always Bendu's day was crowded with chores, a treadmill of survival that kept the palms of her hands split with calluses and back prone to pain. Returning to her room she used some of the water to wash her cooking pot and plate which were still dirty from the night before. Over the charcoal fire she shared with Ma Fata she then cooked herself some rice and mixed it with the last of her palm butter. Storage of cooked food is impossible without power for refrigeration so, like millions of other people in a country without electricity, Bendu rarely prepared more than what could be eaten at one sitting. Ma Fata was clucking around her side of the compound, busy with her own work so now was not the time to discuss dreams. It can wait, thought Bendu.

After sweeping the floor of her hut and her 'side' of the mango tree clearing, she took the water basin behind a screen of woven palm leaves erected over a collection of flagstones she had dragged up from the river bed, and washed herself. Her cheap soap stuck to the stones, making them white and slippy so, as always, she focused on keeping her footing before looking skywards and tipping the final dregs of the water over her forehead, allowing it to cascade over her body. She could see the first blue of the sky as the morning mist lifted and she knew the heat of the day would soon build. Running her hands over her limbs, she flicked off most of the water before putting her lappa back on. By the time she walked the short distance round to her door she was dry.

Wearing her uniform Bendu began the short walk through town to school. There were no tarmac roads in Kailahun and the streets were either dusty in the dry season or muddy when the rains came. At this distance from the capital city, government was merely notional. It did not get much beyond the spreadsheets of aid groups and empty platitudes promised by Freetown politicians, so nobody took care of the roads in Kailahun. Ruts churned up by trucks and jeeps when it rained were baked hard by the sun, creating an assault course that destroyed axles and gearboxes. The only vehicles you saw in Kailahun were either new 4x4 jeeps owned by aid groups or battered local vehicles – minibuses and trucks – with doors missing, shattered windscreens, and bodywork patched with crudely welded pieces of metal.

Bendu had once asked a town councilor at a public meeting held near the remnants of the petrol station in town why, after so many years of international aid, the town of Kailahun was still a ruin. She forgot the first part of his answer which was all about politics but she could not forget the self-important smirk on his face as this man told her not to bother herself with such questions because 'In Africa your elders know best.'

Only 'okadas', the cheap Chinese-made motorbikes used as taxis, could move with any sense of speed as the young, male riders dared to surf the troughs and peaks of the roadway. Each time she walked through town Bendu would have to jump out of the way as the bikes sputtered past in a haze of blue exhaust fumes. The bluer the smoke the dirtier the fuel and, in a town as remote as Kailahun, the fuel was never clean.

She had never trusted the 'okada' men. Most of them were rebels who had been given motorbikes by the United Nations in exchange for laying down their arms. She remembered how once she had climbed on to the back of a bike only to be overwhelmed by an aroma cocktail of palm wine and sweat on the rider that brought back terrible memories. That day was baking hot but by the time she managed to jump off she was covered in goose bumps.

Bendu walked past the ruined mosque, the largest building in town, then past the old mission station that once belonged to the Methodists but was now a store room for general traders. Their old shops destroyed, today's sellers made do with wooden roadside huts that had to be secured each night with iron bars and padlocks. The lack of reliable police in Sierra Leone meant law and order was a service normal people had to provide for themselves. Bendu stopped at what passed for a grocery store – a small shack with a tray out front made from rough planks nailed together – but all the trader had in stock was pasta. He was selling a few pieces at a time, wrapped in a twist of cellophane, for in a town as constitutionally poor as Kailahun few could afford an entire box. She would check on the way home from school to see if any delivery trucks had made it through from Freetown.

The day's first beads of sweat ran down Bendu's face from the rim of her green felt cap as she lined up for registration at 7.30am. School gave her a sense of purpose that she had rarely felt before but if she was honest she never felt particularly comfortable there. After missing out on so many years of schooling, most of her fellow pupils who had not been so caught up in the war were much more advanced than her. She felt it a mark of shame that girls not yet in their teens could recite answers quicker than she could.

And she also bore the physical effects from the war. After so many years walking unshod through the bush, her feet were so spread and swollen it had been agony to put on school shoes for the first time. She could remember the day shortly after arriving at MGH when she took off her shoes to ease the pain and the entire playground had started chanting 'Elephant feet! Elephant feet!' Since then she had kept her shoes on and herself to herself.

On the day after the dream Bendu had taken up her normal position during break time, sitting under the shade of a tree on the edge of a group of classmates, listening but not saying much. Her peers were all sixteen years old and the conversation had returned to a subject that occupied more and more of their time – initiation.

Across West Africa boys become men and girls become women only after a period of training at the hands of traditional societies. In Sierra Leone the bush societies are known as 'Poro' for men and 'Bundu' for women. It is meant to be secret but everybody knew the basics; the young person is taken away under cover of darkness and led deep into the bush where they are kept for weeks, sometimes months, before finally emerging as an adult sworn to uphold the vow of silence about exactly what went on. The imaginations of every generation of West African children have sought to fill in the gaps of what actually happens during the period in the bush societies.

Bendu listened to the excited talk about the girls' upcoming initiations. Mostly they dwelled on the fine new dress the Bundu society traditionally presents to each graduate and how they would then be able to take a husband. Bendu was older than sixteen – quite how much older was unclear as she had never had an official birth certificate – and she found it hard to share the excitement of the others. For her, the idea of being forced to live out in the bush and do the bidding of others reminded her of what had gone on during the war.

It all got too much when one of the girls, Aminatta, began talking casually about the culmination of the female initiation when the student is held down by the senior society members and is cut. Bendu had once heard some foreign aid workers calling it by an abbreviation, FGM, which stood for Female Genital Mutilation. Another, a scientist, described how the clitoris of each girl is removed without any drugs to ease the pain or chemicals to clean the wound or the blade.

'How bad can it be when they do this?' Aminatta asked boastfully. 'My sister told me one of the girls in her group fought and fought. But I will be brave so I can become a proper woman.'

The thought of being cut there made Bendu feel a pit open somewhere below her stomach. She closed her eyes and her mind spun with images of drunken gunmen and UN medical staff in surgical outfits. For a moment she stopped listening to the girls' talk but when her focus returned Aminatta was speaking again, bragging about how her mother and grandmother told her initiation was nothing to worry about. 'In Africa your elders know best,' she said.

The school day finished at 1pm when the cracked bell in the yard was rung but Bendu still had a lot to do. The heat of the day was at its most exhausting but she had to walk back to the traders to see if a truck had made it through to Kailahun. Disappointed, she walked back to her hut, changed out of her school clothes and spent the afternoon fetching, drying and sorting rice.

First she had to walk the two miles out into the forest to where the tiny parcel of land owned by her late father was found. It was called, rather grandly, a field, but it looked like a place where a cyclone had touched down. Half-felled trees lay at drunken angles, fouled by a web of ivy and undergrowth that trapped them in mid-fall. The ground was uneven and there were large rocks everywhere but the fact that the forest canopy had been broken meant sunlight could get through and crops could be grown, mostly mountain rice but also a little cassava. Just on the edge of the field Bendu had erected a rice attic, a small thatched room raised eight feet off the ground on bare branch stilts to save the crop from rats.

Bendu looked in the undergrowth until she found the stout bamboo pole with footholds cut into each side which she used as a ladder. After propping it up against the platform of the attic she climbed up and retrieved a sack of rice. The faded letters of a European aid group were just about legible on the sack as she lowered it down to earth, placed it firmly on her head, hid the ladder and turned for home.

Once back she swept the area outside the hut and spread the rice out to dry while she went to fetch water from the river. She then spent an hour bent double carefully picking out pieces of stalk, grass and rotten rice, all the time shooing away chickens pecking at the grain. She then gathered the rice back up again and began the laborious process of winnowing. Cupful by cupful she poured the rice into a circular tray made of woven grass before flipping the grain up and catching it as it fell. The heavy, healthy grains worked their way to the far edge of the tray, allowing Bendu to remove the chaff which gathered on the near side. It took all afternoon to sort the sack.

At sunset Bendu lit the charcoal fire and cooked a pot of rice. Without salt the meal was difficult to swallow but a few boiled cassava leaves made it at least palatable. By the time Ma Fata had taken her place to cook at the shared hearth Bendu was itching to talk but she knew she had to be patient. Ma Fata's feet were red after a day of treading oil out of half-cooked palm fruit and she seemed a little tired so Bendu deliberately spent longer than usual washing in her open-air bathroom, to allow Ma Fata enough time to eat and relax.

'Ma Fata, please can I ask your help to understand a dream I had last night?' Bendu asked when she got back to the fireplace. The old lady had always treated her with respect, not something Bendu had experienced much of her in life, so the young girl was always polite.

'Of course, child,' the old lady said. 'Let me fetch a chair for us both and we will talk.'

She went back into her hut and re-emerged with two wooden stools. They were crudely made but polished from years of use and very comfortable. Ma Fata half-closed her eyes. She knew a little of Bendu's past in the war and was not surprised to hear her sleep was disturbed. She hoped the recollection would not be too painful for the girl. Precisely and slowly, Bendu recounted everything she could remember from the dream; the screeching noise, the fear of the other girls, the sight of the raffia-cloaked figure, the threatening dance and, most importantly, the calm Bendu felt when she started to confront it.

Ma Fata was silent for a few moments rocking gently on the stool. She did not want to stir bad old memories for a child who had suffered so much but she also knew Bendu was wise enough to catch her out if she held things back. Ma Fata decided to be fully honest.

'What you saw, my child, was a devil.'

Bendu was silent, watching Ma Fata very closely by the glow of the burning charcoal. The old lady continued.

'Not a devil like the ones the missionaries who run your school talk about, but our devil, a bush devil. These are the one who run the secret societies, Bundu and Poro. I am sure you have heard about them even though we are not meant to speak of them.'

Bendu nodded. During her time in the bush during the war there had been plenty of talk about devils.

'When I was a child, a long time ago now, I was taken for initiation and I remember the devil coming on the last day to make sure all the girls behaved themselves. The devil was wearing a mask, just like you describe, and a suit of grass, dancing and screeching. You see, the devils are the ones who keep order, like the teachers at your fancy school. They make sure you do as you are told.'

Bendu thought for a second before asking a question: 'But why do they need to scare people so much? Why do they use fear?'

'It's our traditional way. It's the way we make sure the next generation carries it on. You know in Africa you elders know best.'

As Bendu stared into the fire the flames began to die down but the embers glowed steadily hotter and hotter. She smiled to herself and nodded as her dream steadily began to make sense.

All her life had taught her that surrendering blindly to tradition was the wrong thing to do. The warlords of Sierra Leone stoked years of conflict by drilling children into mindless killers, staking claim to their loyalty because of some spurious representation of African tradition. And politicians allowed their country to wither, pocketing aid money and lathering on layers of graft and nepotistic bureaucracy, with a nudge and wink about it being the way things were done in Africa. It was all right, they made plain, to wait in line and gorge at the trough of embezzlement when one's turn comes. And girls across the country were expected to meekly accept physical assault, to let someone else carve away not only a sensitive part of their anatomy but any true sense of control they have over their destinies, simply because their mother or grandmother had once put up with it.

No, thought Bendu, this was not right. Tradition was one thing but blindly accepting other people's version of tradition was wrong. She would not make the same mistake, she thought. She would stand up to the devil.

The Woman Who Carried a Shop on Her Head

DEBORAH MOGGACH

Deborah Moggach is the author of many successful novels including *These Foolish Things*, *Tulip Fever*, and, most recently, *In the Dark*. Her screenplays include the film of *Pride and Prejudice*, which was nominated for a BAFTA.
She lives in North London.

Ernestine was a tall, sinewy woman who walked miles each day carrying a beauty parlour on her head. This was a heavy wooden box, open at the front, packed with all the products a female might need to make herself desirable – face creams, hair accessories, soap, make-up, skin lighteners, conditioners, razors, hair removal foam, kirby grips and ornaments, perfumes and body lotions. Ernestine sold these in the local villages, tramping along footpaths in her dusty flip-flops, stopping at the secondary school at two-thirty to catch the girls when they came out, working the crossroads where each Thursday the buses disgorged the women returning from market. Though dealing in beauty, Ernestine herself was the least vain of women. Back in her house there was a small, cracked mirror propped on a shelf but she seldom had time to look at it. Besides, when night fell it was too dark to see anything much as they had no electricity. And besides, her husband seemed happy with her as she was.

Or so she believed.

He was a good man, you see. A devout churchgoer, like herself; a hard-working father to their children. Unlike so many men, oh so many, he had never strayed, or even expressed the slightest interest in another woman. They had been married for seventeen years and never, not once, had she regretted leaving her family home in the north, beside the great lake with its drowned trees. The trees were drowned when they built the dam and her little brothers used to make money swimming through the underwater forest, unpicking the nets that had tangled in the branches. Ernestine dreamed about the lake, about the sun sinking over the water and beneath it the fish swimming between the tree-trunks but she had no desire to return to her childhood, she had her own children now. She was exhausted by working hard to keep them in school, to give them the opportunity of a better life than hers, but she loved them and was loved, the Lord be praised, and Kwesi was a good man. Or so she thought.

The night before it happened, the Wednesday night, Grace came home late. Grace was the eldest of Ernestine's daughters, a studious young woman of sixteen. She was tall and big-boned, like her mother, with a square jaw and an uncompromising stare through her spectacles. She worked hard at school and in the evenings, when the village was plunged into darkness, she toiled at her homework under one of the few spots of illumination, the strip light that bathed with a bluish glow the fried-fish stall at the side of the road. People stopped to gossip with her auntie, who ran it, but Grace kept her head down, she was uninterested in tittle-tattle, she was fierce in her determination to pass her exams and go to college. Not for her the girlish giggles at school, the huddled whisperings about boys and lipstick. Grace was above such things; indeed, she had recently been elected Team Leader of the Abstinence Programme, its slogan *Just Say No*. She lectured her fellow teenagers on the perils of premarital sex and the way that early parenthood destroyed all hopes of a future career. She led the singing, '*Boys boys boys take care of girls girls girls*', and promoted, as an alternative to temptation, the taking up of vigorous sports and the reading of improving texts.

All in all she was an admirable young woman. Ernestine was proud of her – how could she not be? Sometimes, however, she felt awed by her daughter, and sometimes she feared for the girl whose rigid convictions were so untempered by the rough complexities of life. And Grace was not the easiest person to live with; recently she had grown short-tempered, as if her own family, even her little brothers and sisters, were included in the congregation of sinners.

That evening she was particularly irritable, and snapped at her granny for forgetting to wash her football shirt. There was a match the next day with the team from the Asseweya High School. She gave no explanation for her late return and disappeared into the bedroom she shared with her sisters. Ernestine, at the time, presumed she was frustrated by the earlier power cut that had plunged their village into darkness for two hours and stopped her from doing her homework. Ernestine was not an interfering mother and besides, with a family as large as hers there were always plenty of squabbles, particularly amongst the girls. The boys just fought. For sure it was hard work surviving day to day with eight mouths to feed but the Lord had blessed them with good health and despite their worries they had much to be thankful for. Many of Ernestine's customers were women struggling to bring up their families alone, their husbands working a long way from home, or passed away, or gone off gallivanting with another woman. One of them had taken a seventeen-year-old girl as his second wife, would you believe, a man of forty-three, and had moved to Nigeria, leaving his children fatherless.

For sure, Ernestine was blessed to have Kwesi for a husband.

The next day, Thursday, was market day at Asseweya, their local town. Kwesi travelled there each week to sell the plantains and pineapples he grew on his land; on that particular day Ernestine accompanied him as she had to buy new stock from the wholesaler.

On market day the town was jammed with traffic –

buses, trucks, *tro-tros* burdened with sacks of produce. Hawkers crowded around them selling crisps, bananas, Bibles, fried snacks, fizzy drinks, Arsenal t-shirts, selling everything under the sun. Ernestine recognised Mustafa, the little son of her neighbour, his head weighed down with a bowl of plastic water-sachets which he passed to the outstretched hands. He choked in the fumes: he had asthma, but his mother, a widow, could neither afford medicine nor afford to send him to school. Ernestine felt sorry for the six-year-old and grateful, yet again, that her children knew their alphabet and had a father who took care of them and sang hymns beside them in church.

Kwesi left his mobile at the phone-charging booth before disappearing into the crowd of the market-place. Every week he left his mobile there and picked it up in the afternoon, before going home. The phone-charger, Ngobo, sat behind his array of mobiles. Ernestine had never seen him moving from his position; he had sharp eyes that missed nothing; there was something about him that made her uneasy. She could feel him watching her as she negotiated her way through the traffic to God Is Good Beauty Products, on the other side of the road.

Ernestine enjoyed her visits to Lily, who ran the business. They sat in the back room, the ceiling fan whirring, drinking Fanta and gossiping. Lily told her about the latest scandals, whose husband had run away with whose wife, whose daughter had become pregnant. That particular day she told Ernestine a story about two little girls who were tricked into having the Dipo, the initiation rite, but who escaped, jumping onto a *tro-tro* and hiding amongst the passengers. As Lily talked, her eyes widened and her breathing quickened. Ernestine was enthralled; dramas in the town seemed so much larger than those in her own sleepy village. Little did she suspect the drama brewing just a few yards away.

It happened like this. At the end of the day, when the market was packing up, Kwesi was still busy so Ernestine went to collect his mobile phone. Ngobo paused before giving it back.

'I have something to tell you, madam,' he said, his voice hoarse. She smelt alcohol on his breath. 'It's not pleasant, but I feel it is my duty.' He gazed at the mobile in his hand. 'I sit here, you see. I sit here and watch the world go by. There's things I see.' He paused, breathing heavily. 'It concerns your husband and a *certain female*.'

He looked up at her, waiting for her reaction. She didn't speak.

He passed her the mobile. 'So when it's juiced up again it beeps, that means it's got a message.' Ngobo gave her a sorrowful look. 'It's you I was thinking of.'

'What do you mean?' she whispered.

'What do I mean, dear lady? I mean, I pressed the button and I listened to what the message said.'

*

Ernestine sat jammed against her husband in the bus. She couldn't speak; she felt emptied of breath. Kwesi said nothing either but then he was a man of few words. His silence today, however, now she knew the truth, seemed pregnant with guilt. His bony shoulder and hip pressed against her – the bus was jammed with people – but now it felt like an alien body, a body that belonged to someone else.

Her brain felt sluggish, drugged with shock. The questions turned over and over, laboriously. How could he do such a thing? How long had it been going on? How often had it happened? How could be betray her, and his children? How could he?

The woman's name was Adwoa and Ernestine knew her well. In fact Adwoa Shaibu-Ali was one of her best customers. She lived at the far end of the village and was a buxom, handsome, lazy woman with a brood of illiterate children, for Adwoa kept the girls at home to look after the babies that she produced at regular intervals and to do the housework which she was too indolent to do herself. Her thin, elderly husband worked uncomplainingly to keep her in the style to which she was accustomed – new make-up, new clothes, a monthly visit to Asseweya to get her hair-weaves put in. Few of the local women could afford the hairdresser and they wrapped their heads in cloths but Adwoa's hair was always glossy, a curvy bob, ornamented with a selection of Ernestine's novelty clips.

Most of the day Adwoa sat around nattering to her neighbours, leafing through magazines and pausing only to cuff one of her children. And texting on her mobile. She was always texting.

The sun was setting by the time Ernestine got home. Normally it was her favourite time of day. Up in the trees the bats detached themselves from the bat-clumps that hung down like heavy bundles of fruit; they flew off, one by one, into the suffused sky. Today they looked sinister with their leather wings and sharp little teeth. Everything had turned upside down; it was as if Ernestine had plunged into the lake of her childhood, plunged beneath the placid surface, and found herself in a strange and menacing world, a warped reflection of the real one that she had so foolishly taken for granted.

It was still stiflingly hot. She watched Kwesi as he washed himself in a bowl of water. His chest was bare, his hair dripping. He wasn't a handsome man, his nose was too big and his ears stuck out, but he was hers, and they had been man and wife for half her lifetime. Beside him, the unsuspecting Grace was stirring *banku* over the fire. She looked so pure, so innocent. Kwesi's mother was chopping onions. Old and frail, she doted on her son. What was going to happen to their family, that a few hours ago had seemed so contented?

Night fell. Nobody noticed Ernestine's silence; she had never been a chatty woman. She moved around in a daze, the voices of her family echoing far away. She was more hurt than angry – hurt, and deeply humiliated, that her husband had revealed himself to be no better than all those other men, the errant fornicators whose wives she used to pity. How blind she had been! In bed she lay rigid beside him, and when he put his hand on her breast she muttered that she was tired and turned away. Soon he fell asleep but for many hours she lay awake, her mind racing. What was she going to do – tell him she knew all about his affair with Adwoa? Kick him out of their home? The prospect was too terrifying, it made her blood run cold. Beside her slept her youngest boys, the twins. What would they do, without a father? And what would Grace do, a budding young woman, filled with such purity and fervour, when she discovered that her father was an adulterer?

The next day Ernestine went to the monthly meeting of the women's savings group. In normal times she looked forward to this; the twelve women had formed a close bond based on mutual trust and a shared stake in each other's financial matters; besides, it was a chance to catch up on each other's news. Ernestine was proud, that she had saved up her money each month to start her own business, that as a respected member of the community she now held one of the keys to the money box. Today, however, she was filled with dread. As they sat in a circle under the trees, she looked at the faces around her. Did any of them know? Did the whole village know, and had everyone been whispering behind her back? Would she soon be like Dede, the widowed mother of little Mustafa the water-seller, who lived in such abject poverty that she could only contribute one *cedi* a month and had frequently been bailed out by the other women, much to her shame?

Adwoa didn't belong to the group; she was a stranger to thrift and female empowerment, she let her husband do the work while she sat at home on her big bottom, leaving messages to Ernestine's husband on her mobile phone. Ernestine wondered what Adwoa was doing – primping herself up for a tryst with Kwesi? Rubbing Imam Shea Butter on to her skin and anointing her lips with the Yana Luxury Lip Shimmer she had bought the week before, the better to kiss him with? Ernestine felt sick. Kwesi's patch of land was not far from Adwoa's house; was it there that they met, hidden amongst the cassava bushes? Ernestine hadn't heard the message, Ngobo had deleted it to save her blushes, he said, but the gist of it seemed to be how much Adwoa was longing to see her Kwesi again, she could hardly wait. *Her* Kwesi.

Now Ernestine thought of it, Adwoa's youngest baby had a big nose, just like Kwesi's.

'Are you ready?'

Ernestine jumped. The two other key-holders were waiting. Ernestine rallied and the three women opened the padlocks. They all sang a song together, gathered round the tin box and got down to business. Dede, whose husband had died of AIDS, was saving up for a piece of land to grow maize. Humu was supporting herself through school by running a food stall. Lydia was setting up a biscuit bakery. Ernestine gazed at the scene – the dappled shadows, the chickens scratching in the dust, the kids walking from one woman to another, selling sweets and plantain chips. Her secret weighed her down; she had a strong urge to confide in somebody.

There was a burst of laughter. Nancy and Irene sat together, sharing a joke. They also shared a husband, Joseph. Two years earlier, when Joseph had taken the young Irene as his second wife, all hell had broken loose. The savings club, however, had brought them together. Previously both women had made a meagre living selling cassava, which they chopped laboriously by hand, paying a middle-man for the milling. But with the help of the tin box they had clubbed together to buy a milling machine and now they worked it together, joking about Joseph's shortcomings as the machine whirred away. Could Ernestine ever imagine sharing her husband with another woman?

The idea was disgusting. She would rather die. Later, back home, she inspected her face in the mirror. It gazed back at her, naked, square-jawed. She had never worn make-up. Perhaps she should use some of her own products to woo Kwesi back. She could pluck her eyebrows and lighten her skin with Dimples Skin Lightener. She could perfume herself with jasmine and use her Cote D'Azur make-up kit, complete with brushes, to shadow her eyes and paint her lips. Maybe then she could win back his love.

Or she could visit Giti, the witch. Everyone feared Giti. She lived alone behind the mosque, she was known to have the evil eye. Only the other week a headless chicken had been found outside her front door. Giti could put a curse on one of Ernestine's skin creams. When Adwoa bought it, her face would erupt in boils and Kwesi would run away in horror.

What else could Ernestine do? She could go to church and pray. She could storm into Adwoa's house and tell her to lay off her husband. She could have a showdown with Kwesi.

Or she could do nothing and hope it would pass.

Ernestine was a coward; she did nothing. The sun sank behind the trees. The bats detached themselves and flew away. She swept the floor and washed her mother-in-law's hair. She separated her squabbling sons. Her older children came home from school. She cooked them *jollof* rice and red pepper sauce. Her husband came home from the fields and put his mobile on the shelf, where it always sat. Grace came home, her books under her arm. She didn't say a word. Ernestine caught Grace looking at herself and Kwesi with an odd expression on her face. Did she know something was up?

*

The days passed. Ernestine went out selling her wares but she avoided Adwoa's house, she couldn't bear to see the woman. On Wednesday the girls' football team played a match and Ernestine, working the crowd, made a large number of sales. Grace had backed out of the match saying she didn't feel well. She was nowhere to be seen, and wasn't at home when Ernestine returned. At the time Ernestine thought nothing of it, presuming Grace was menstruating. She had too many other things on her mind.

The next morning, needing to replenish her stock, she rose early, to travel into Asseweya with her husband. It was hard to believe that only a week had passed since her last visit.

The sun was rising as they climbed into the bus. It was just pulling into the road when someone yelled.

'Wait!'

Ernestine looked out of the window. Adwoa hobbled towards them, one hand clutching her long, tight skirt, the other hand waving the bus to stop.

Adwoa squeezed herself into the seat behind them. She was dressed in an orange and green batik outfit; her hair was embellished with one of Ernestine's gardenia-clips, and she was perspiring from the unaccustomed exercise.

Ernestine froze. The harlot greeted Kwesi politely, as if she hardly knew him – she nodded to him as she nodded to the other passengers from the village. Her mascara was smudged and she was breathing heavily.

She leaned forward to Ernestine. 'My dear, I'm spitting mad,' she muttered. 'I've got a bone to pick with my brother, the good-for-nothing drunk.'

Ernestine's head span. She glanced at her husband but now the bus was moving he appeared to have dozed off. It was all pretence, of course.

Adwoa was jabbering away. It seemed to be a family quarrel about a will. '. . . left him some land but he can't farm it, the rascal's a cripple! . . .' The words seemed to come from far off. Ernestine's mind was busy. Was this a pre-arranged tryst between her husband and Adwoa? After all, it was unusual for her, Ernestine, to go to Asseweya two weeks running. The two fornicators were certainly playing a clever game, Kwesi feigning sleep and his mistress engaging Ernestine in some incomprehensible story about a drunken cripple.

When they arrived in town Adwoa pushed her way to the front of the bus. Ernestine watched her big, gaudy body work its way through the crowd. She was heading for the phone-charging booth.

And now Adwoa was standing there, shouting at Ngobo, the man with the mobiles, the man who never moved. The man who, it turned out, happened to be her brother.

*

People said it was God's will, that Ngobo was born a cripple. People said it was an ancestral curse. People said it was just bad luck. Some people had shown him kindness; some had bullied him. Mostly, however, people had ignored him. When he was a child he had begged at the crossroads outside Asseweya, where the traffic streamed between Accra and the north. Every day one of his brothers or sisters would push him along the central reservation and leave him at the traffic lights. He sat on his little cart, his withered legs tucked beneath him. This was a prime spot for the disabled and fights would break out between them as they jostled for the best position.

But the worst fights were with his sister, Adwoa.

Adwoa, who throughout his childhood bullied and teased him. Who stole his sweets and ran away on her strong healthy legs. Who ridiculed him to the other girls. Who left him on his cart, in the rain, while she disappeared into the bushes with her boyfriends. Who stole his money and taunted him to come and get it. And who now was trying to steal back a cassava-patch their father had left to him in his will.

A cripple has to develop alternative methods of survival. Over the years, Ngobo had learnt to be wily. Of course he was bitter – how could he not be? But he had his wits. Each day, at his stall, he watched people coming and going, busy with their day, blessed with their children, people who took it for granted that they could move from one place to another, dance, have sex, have a life.

All Ngobo had were his mobile phones. They sat there on his table, rows of them, plugged in and silently charging. Within them lay the only power he had – the power to settle old feuds, to pay back his tormenters . . . And to make mischief.

*

How did Ernestine discover the truth – that Ngobo had lied, that there was no message on her husband's phone, that Ngobo had simply wanted to take revenge on his sister? Why had he chosen Ernestine and her husband, a respectable, hard-working couple who loved each other? What had they ever done to him?

I'll never know because at this point the trail grows cold. I suspect that Ernestine's strong, unadorned beauty had inflamed him, that he was half in love with her himself, and bitterly jealous of her happy marriage. That he had watched her on her visits to the beauty shop on the other side of the road, and wanted her for himself. Who knows? I heard the story from Lily, who owned God Is Good Beauty Products. She's my cousin, and I dropped in on her when I travelled to Ghana to visit my relatives.

All I heard was that a few days later Ernestine's daughter Grace, who had been acting so strangely, drew her mother aside and told her that she was expecting a baby. The father was a taxi-driver who used to stop at her auntie's stall to eat her fried fish. He had promised to marry Grace but he was never seen again. Poor Grace, so rigid and intransigent, and who, it transpires, didn't manage to practise what she preached.

When I arrived in Accra I stayed at the Novotel. They put me on the second floor. Through my window I could see the pool, the sunbathers, the waiters serving drinks amongst the bougainvilleas. A high wall surrounded the garden.

When I returned from upcountry they put me on the sixth floor. This was above the wall and when I looked out of the window a different Africa was spread below me: the Makola Market which stretched as far as the eye could see . . . a heaving mass of people, vegetables, goats. The room was air-conditioned and the window sealed, but in my heart I could hear the voices and the music, I could smell the exhaust fumes and the frying food. . . .

I watched it for hours as the sun set and the swallows swooped. And then it was gone, as if it had never been. When night falls Africans melt back into the darkness, into their unknowable lives. Then the hotel reception rang to tell me my taxi had arrived, to take me to the airport.

Africa evaporated into the blaze of the terminal building. All I had was Lily's shea butter, which I rubbed into my hands. I smelt it on my skin as I slept all the way back to England, leaving Ghana, and her stories, behind.

Ovarian Roulette

KATHY LETTE

Kathy Lette first achieved *succès de scandale* as a teenager with the novel *Puberty Blues*. After several years as a newspaper columnist and television sitcom writer in America and Australia, she wrote ten international bestsellers including *Foetal Attraction, Mad Cows, How to Kill Your Husband (and other handy household hints)* and *To Love, Honour and Betray*. Her novels have been published in fourteen languages around the world. Two have been made into motion pictures. She lives in London with her husband and two children and has recently been awarded an Honorary Doctorate by Southampton University.

Brazil is a Catholic country, so copulation equals population. What about the Rhythm Method, I hear you ask? Well, do you know what you call a woman who uses the Rhythm Method? Mum.

I'm in Brazil. I know. It's a long way to go for a wax. In fact I'm in the equivalent of an unwaxed pudenda – the north east of the country, Maranhao, on the edge of the rainforest, home to the country's poorest people. I'm not actually here for a Brazilian (this is the only context in which you'll ever hear me say this, but Bring Back Bush!) but to see what Plan is doing to improve the lives of young women in this impoverished place.

I wanted to tell the story of one girl. But all the girls I met – Maria, Jeanine, Rosana, Lorena, Amanda, Marina, Cintia, Melissa, Nataly, Teresa, Ana and Johanna – had the same sad tale. It's a story of child prostitution, teenage pregnancy, HIV, no contraception, illegal back-street abortion, sex tourism, single mothers, macho men, irresponsible, absentee fathers and domestic violence.

*

Teresa is typical. She is fifteen and already has two baby girls. Her sisters fell pregnant at twelve and fourteen respectively. The question is, did they *fall*, or were they *pushed*? With no access to contraceptives and brash, cocksure boyfriends who refuse to wear condoms, especially when deflowering a girl – it's a game of Ovarian Roulette.

A pregnancy test is the one test you can't cheat on – and these teenagers fail it far too regularly. The placenta is known locally as 'the partner' – and in most cases, it's the only partner there at the birth. The fathers are U.F.Os: Unidentified Fleeing Objects. Brazilian men seem to approach commitment with the same enthusiasm a nude guy approaches a barbed-wire fence. To them a 'paternity suit' is the latest look in men's leisure wear down in Rio.

The town I am visiting, São Luís, is nick-named 'The Love Island', because of the high number of pregnant teenagers and AIDS patients. The slum where Teresa lives is called, ironically, the Olympic Village, *Cidade Olimpica*. 70,000 people squat here in destitution – going for Gold in the Misery Olympics. With fetid garbage strewn on every street corner, no running water but plenty of running raw sewage and decrepit buildings scarred in graffiti, you could say that on first view, the favelas lack charm. On second and third sight too, actually. But the charm of the women I met made up for it. Despite their penury, in each ramshackle dwelling young abandoned teenage mothers greeted me with shy generosity and warmth.

Teresa invited me into the minuscule hut she shares with her mum and two children. It's a lopsided mud-brick construction which leans tipsily into the street. The holes in the walls are stuffed with plastic bags to keep out the rain and wind. A sardine would feel cramped in there. And yet, clean washing fluttered from lines which criss-crossed the tiny room. Her two little girls, eighteen months and three, sported perfectly plaited hair and freshly laundered frocks.

I asked the teenager if she would like to go back to school. 'Oh, I would love to,' she replied, despondently, 'but there is nobody to look after my kids.' Her first unwanted pregnancy forced her to leave school.

The door wheezed open and Teresa's mother shuffled in unexpectedly from work. World-weary and weather-beaten, she looked eighty, but is only forty. Teresa shyly revealed that her mother was also pregnant at twelve. I asked Teresa's mum if it was difficult to accept that her three daughters became mothers at such a tender age, just as she did.

'It is difficult to accept, yes. I was very sad when I found out my daughters were pregnant. But the reason . . . well, their father was not a good example.' Sadness strained her face as she lowered her bulk on to the bed next to me, the springs mourning beneath us. 'He drank and smoked a lot of dope in the house. Both girls were rebellious and angry that I stayed living with this man. It's been very difficult for them.' She was fretting at her fingers, bending and stretching them as if warming up for a piano concerto. 'You see, my own mother, had three children by the time she was sixteen. They were starving. At ten years old, I was the eldest so I became a prostitute to bring home milk for the baby and food for my siblings. I didn't want to steal. I would rather work as a prostitute,' she said defiantly, the veins in her neck standing out like cables.

'I took drugs to numb the experience. My boyfriend, he was thirteen years old, he took drugs too. He became an addict. At fifteen my boyfriend was living off me as a pimp. He use to hit me.' Her face burned with indignation. 'I have been a victim of domestic violence all my life.' Tears ran down her lined, exhausted face. 'I am most ashamed of the time I had to have three men at once,' she admitted, her face as crumpled as the unmade beds she is trying to forget.

I felt dreadful that my questions had made her weep. I tried to change conversational tack, explaining, self-deprecatingly that with my diplomacy skills I really should take up a career in hostage negotiations . . . But Teresa's mother waved away my apologies and insisted on concluding her confession. 'This year I've accepted Jesus and found the strength to leave prostitution and my pimp,' she revealed, her voice see-sawing with emotion. She is telling me all this, she said, 'because Jesus tells us to embrace the truth'. (Teresa's mother has abandoned Catholicism for the Pentecostal religion – an increasing trend in Brazil.)

She started to cry again, blaming herself for her daughters' blighted lives. 'It was so bad at home, the drinking, the violence, it was no wonder my girls went wild.' Thick tears plopped onto her chapped hands.

Teresa, mortified with embarrassment at her mother's unexpected revelations, plugged a squawking baby with a bottle and looked at her feet. I probed the mother a little more, enquiring why she hadn't talked to her daughters about contraception. Ironically, although working as a prostitute, her Catholic upbringing had left her too self-conscious to broach such sinful subjects. Her only advice to her three daughters had been, 'don't go out with boys'. She admitted that it is now something she bitterly regrets. 'We just feel ashamed to talk about these issues.'

In a rather bleak postscript, she concluded that in the Plan-run school where she now works as a cleaner, she can see the twelve- and-thirteen-year-old girls going with men for money. She had worked as a child prostitute to support her own mother who had also worked as a child prostitute and both had endured pregnancies aged eleven. And now her three daughters have followed biological suit by having babies in their early teens. It's a vicious cycle – a menstrual cycle. The question is, how to break it? Teresa's mother receives no alimony or social security. She must work scrubbing floors all day to support her three daughters and clutch of grandchildren, even though her hands are gnarled with arthritis. She sleeps in a hammock strung across the dismal room; her daughters and their babies nestled into the small cots below.

In Brazil, paedophile tourism is rife. (In São Luís alone, 1,000 children are known to have been sexually exploited in the last year.) The young girls I met told me of specific bars and service stations where such tourists go, knowing that children will be available for proposition. One of Plan's counsellors revealed that even though the government says they're trying to break these paedophile rings, the girls are getting younger. 'They use to be twelve to seventeen. It's now eight- to nine-year-olds being offered, with younger children pimped by their parents, in their own homes. Two weeks ago,' she added, bleakly, 'a father and grandfather were convicted of having sex with the youngest child in the family – she is four – and of selling her to men. The little girls have to be stitched up as their vaginas have been torn and split. Sometimes they are also penetrated with objects. I see these cases every day and I never get used to it.'

In every dilapidated shack, I found young women who had become little more than a life support to their ovaries – reduced, by lack of contraception and lack of access to abortion, into breeding cows. Forced to drop out of school and unable to work, it's as though society has handed them an eviction notice. They have become runners-up in the human race. Cintia and her sister share a hovel with their four babies and their mother, who, although also crippled with arthritis, must work as a domestic to support them – yet is paid only at the whim of her mistress. As there is high unemployment, no unions and no basic wage, Cintia's mother has no choice but to put up with this capriciousness and take the fiscal scraps she is thrown.

At fourteen, Cintia had a baby, prematurely. 'I wanted to be a police woman,' she told me, with longing. Her sister, now eighteen and the mother of three children, with another on the way, wanted to be a teacher. But instead they look after their babies and try to help their mother around the house. 'Mum was angry with us at first, but loves us and the kids.'

But how can these mothers mother, when they so desperately need to be mothered themselves?

Although their shack is neat and tidy, there is no money for a septic tank. The toilet is a pit covered by two wobbly planks through which the toddlers could easily fall. The sisters dug a hole in the backyard, but had no money to buy a tank. Ignorant about hygiene, they now throw their garbage into the pit – nappies, food scraps and waste – where it all festers in the sun. As it's been raining, the squalid pit has filled with water, turning it into a surreal fishpond in which the soiled nappies bob about. All the babies have rashes, sores and skin complaints, which I can't quite put my finger on – and would much rather not, come to think of it. But there's little doubt that it's to do with the festering bucolic pool in their microscopic yard.

My next visit was to Diana's tumbledown hut. She is thirty with three teenage children. Here the family defecates in a bucket. The mother then wraps the family's faeces in a plastic bag and carries them to the garbage truck once a week. This is the tropics, I hasten to add. She does this week in, week out, year after year after – well, you get the pathetic picture. A case of *Oh, those old familiar faeces*.

Diana's thirteen-year-old daughter sat mutely in the corner, sucking her thumb. Her legs were covered in bites and discolorations. She is four months pregnant. 'As a mother, I do what I can,' Diana shrugged, 'but in these areas, girls start their sexual lives at twelve.'

Diana's daughter told me in a faltering voice that girls have sex so as not to lose a boyfriend. With a self-esteem that is limbo low, they dread being cast off into social Siberia. This macho society encourages young boys to sow whole acres of wild oats, but girls can't go on the pill without parental permission. Most don't have the fifty cents for a packet of three condoms. Many girls die from illegal abortions. They try to abort using herbal pessaries and potions from the forest. The latest misguided fad is for the pregnant girl to eat four ulcer pills and insert four vaginally to provoke miscarriage. 'You can't have babies any more after this,' Diana told me, matter-of-factly.

Worse than the urban slums are the favelas on the edge of the rainforest. The aptly named Poverty Street, Rua de Pobreza, is a cluster of rickety mud houses, with no sanitation and nothing but sheets of plastic tacked to the roof for protection against the five months of rainy season. Half collapsed and open to the elements, the huts look as though Pavarotti has sat on them. There are 4,000 families squatting in this one area, quite literally, as there are no latrines. It must be impossible to get to sleep here – mainly because some insect is always blinking its 9,000,624,439,002 eyes at you in the dark.

Despite this, the young mothers showed me their lean-to's with the pride of 1950s housewives – the tiny stone fireplace for cooking rice, the well where they fetch water, the palm fronds tied together to make a private place to wash, the earthen floors swept clean.

I had come to meet thirteen-year-old Maria, a beautiful and bright student. Her mother asked me to stay for lunch, offering piranha. Gritting my teeth, I decided that I'd better eat it before it ate me, giving a new definition to 'fast food'. What an innovative way to lose weight – eat piranha and diet from the inside!

In a water-to-wine, loaves-and-fishes act which would put Martha Stewart to shame, Maria's mother magicked up a lunch of rice, black-eyed beans, beetroot, tomato, potato and fried fish. The kids stood around wide-eyed, amazed at this sumptuous feast. Starved stray cats insinuated themselves into the hut, weaving a mewling minuet round our legs. Some days the family has nothing to eat, Maria's mum revealed. The adults sleep on a single, lumpy mattress on frayed, torn sheets, the babies in filthy cribs with the other kids strung above them in a hammock. Maria's mother told me that they moved here to try to improve their lives. (How bad could it have been in the city? I wondered, aghast.)

Despite the desperate poverty, there is a quiet dignity to these women. After lunch, I retreated on to Maria's small bed, with her mum and sister, away from the village men. The males hovered nearby, suspiciously. They all had the sort of faces you usually associate with Crime and Accident reconstruction units and I didn't want to rile them.

Maria is doing well at school. She takes pride in her appearance. Two filthy dolls are decoratively draped upon the bed and a plastic handbag is proudly displayed, on a nail on the wall, along with dog-eared books. Her bedsheet depicted a beaming Jesus, but the mattress beneath was just a pile of bricks with a thin blanket. If Maria can over-ride her ovaries, this girl could make her mark. If not, she will join the millions of other young women in the Missing Persons Bureau. And who is missing? The girl with potential – the girl she was B.C. (Before Childbirth).

Out of earshot of the men, I asked Maria's mother what aspirations she has for her daughter. 'To stop her from having a baby,' she told me, emphatically. Maria's mum then whispered that, after a Plan workshop, she started secretly taking the pill. Her sister is operating a similar subterfuge. They dare not tell their husbands. Both women yearn to have their fallopian tubes tied. I asked why their husbands wouldn't go for the snip, being a much simpler operation. Maria's mum shrugged. 'It's impossible to convince my husband to wear a condom, let alone have a vasectomy,' she sighed.

So, what is Plan doing to help these brave women of Brazil? A better question would be, what are they *not* doing? Education, sanitation, nutrition, child protection, literacy workshops, health centres offering free contraception, after-school theatre workshops and football coaching to get kids off the streets – Plan immerse themselves in communities, building long term support and empowering people to fulfil their potential and improve their lives. When it was discovered that Maria and her friends were not attending school as it was too far away, Plan built a school nearby. It is here that the children often get their only meal of the day. (The school has two shifts, one from 7am to 1pm, another from 1pm to 5pm.) In 2007, only 79.2% of children in the north-east of Brazil completed primary school. Brazil has the largest population of under six-year-olds in the Americas.

Plan trains teachers and community volunteers to help young children learn to read. They work with the Brazilian government on eradicating child labour, and providing emergency shelter and food when mud slides destroy communities during the wet season. For the past two years, Plan has been encouraging communities to develop allotments to grow food. In this part of Brazil, young children are fed a staple diet of mingau, a watery porridge made from farine, a starchy flour with low nutritional value. Now families are growing beans, vegetables and herbs like parsley, a spoonful of which every day has enough vitamin A to sustain a child.

There is so much violence in the favelas that children are not safe on the streets. And yet at home, domestic violence against the women and children is astronomically high. With much police corruption (people had told me that if you see a policeman in Brazil – run) Plan's counsellors, elected by other locals, can be an alternative source of intervention, offering shelter and help.

Without the support of Plan, standing up to the macho Brazilian men, a corrupt police force and the patriarchal

Catholic Church would be like facing up to Darth Vader with a butter knife.

As pregnancy consigns many Brazilian women to poverty, it seems clear that Catholicism kills. The dying process begins the moment we come into the world, but it sure speeds up if you are poor in Brazil. Two hundred and twenty-five children under the age of five die every day in Brazil. Thirty-one per cent of family houses in urban areas don't have access to basic sanitation which results in 2,500 deaths a year of children under five as a consequence of the contamination of the water by fecal matter. The number of young murder victims grew five-fold in the last twenty years. Nearly fifty youths are murdered every day. 17,312 youths aged between fifteen and twenty-four years were murdered in 2006.

The Pope promotes abstinence. Well, yes, of course, the one hundred percent safe oral contraceptive is the word 'no'. But with child prostitution and rape rife, this is not an option. Termination is illegal, so when women go to the hospital bleeding from a self-administered abortion, the doctors must report them to the police. One hundred women are currently awaiting trial on self-abortion charges. Recently, a nine-year-old girl was raped by her stepfather. She became pregnant with twins. The Bishop for Pernambuco swore to excommunicate the family and the doctors if they aborted the foetus. And yet it's clear the sanctity of life stops the moment the baby is born – after that the Catholic Church chickens out of its obligations to those eggs. It fails to protect the children its policies have brought into the world, particularly all the little girls who have been pimped by their poverty-stricken parents or left to starve by an indifferent state.

Brazil is a patriarchal society. The girls must get up at six and help their mothers prepare breakfast. The sons get an extra lie-in. When the kids come home from school, the boys play soccer. The girls must help with domestic chores. Seventy-eight per cent of the population believe that domestic violence will go unpunished. During my time in Brazil, everyone was on swine flu alert. But Brazilian women have dated so many swine, even married one or two, and confessed to others in church, that they must surely be immune?

But even so, the spirit of the young Brazilian women I met shone through. Their joy and optimism in the face of adversity made my heart expand like an accordion. Every child I met had the sort of neon smile that made you wish you were wearing Polaroids. When I went swimming with some of the girls from the favela, they giggled uncontrollably at my conservative one-piece swimming costume and my unwaxed pudenda. Even though there is no money for waxing, the girls do trim. (Brazilians are obsessed with deforestation. The rainforest doesn't stand a chance!) I retorted that I liked my pubic hair – that it was like having a little pet in my pants at which they roared with laughter, teasing me mercilessly. I may not wax, but I will wax lyrical about the resilient, beautiful young women of Brazil.

Ballad of a Cambodian Man

XIAOLU GUO

Xiaolu Guo was born in 1973 in south China. She studied film at the Beijing Film Academy and published six books in China before she moved to London in 2002. The English translation of *Village of Stone* (Chatto, 2004) was shortlisted for the *Independent* Foreign Fiction Prize and nominated for the International IMPAC Dublin Literary Award. Her first novel written in English, *A Concise Chinese-English Dictionary for Lovers* (Chatto, 2007) was shortlisted for the Orange Broadband Prize for Fiction. *UFO In Her Eyes* (Chatto, 2009) is her latest novel. Xiaolu's film-making career continues to flourish: Her feature *She, A Chinese* received a Golden Leopard Award at the Locarno Film Festival (2009), and *How is Your Fish Today?* (2006) was selected for the Sundance Festival and awarded the prize for best fiction feature at the Créteil International Women's Film Festival.

The old policeman stepped into the muddy rainwater streaming through the market. A smell of rotted durian fruit hung thickly in the air. He walked fast, with a sad joy, constantly colliding with busy shoppers, driven on by his eagerness to get home. He had to fix his rotten motorbike as soon as possible, and then drive to a village fifteen miles away before sunset.

Dara, or 'the old policeman', as the locals called him, was not really old. He had only just hit fifty, but was still the oldest in his police office. In Siem Reap, or in any of the big towns in Cambodia, apart from those who became bosses, all the older policemen were either retired or had no need to work anymore, thanks to the pocket money they got from bribes. But Dara was still there, and had been for half his life, carrying a gun in northern Cambodia. He was neither rich nor particularly poor, and he was reasonably kind to people, if they weren't discouraged by his silence and often grumpy, motionless face. Dara was, after all, a man with a secret, and an inscrutable dignity. He barely talked about his past; some people said that he had been a soldier when he was young. But his short, solid body showed none of the usual signs, unlike others who had lost their limbs to mines during the war.

Right now, the old policeman was trying to finish his shift without incident, though a small riot was stirring up in the food market; a mango seller was fighting with a motorcycle-taxi man. The latter had blindly ridden into the seller's papayas and mangos, which were laid on a piece of flat cloth on the dirt road, and now the fruits were crushed into a mess. The old policeman heard the seller asking for 5,000 riel in compensation, but the taxi man only cursed her. When he was tired of cursing, he pulled his motorcycle away. Dara knew the man well – he had arrested him twice for heroin trafficking some years ago. But with the intense noon sun heating up the day, the old policeman had no desire to help with anything or arrest anyone. He walked between the customers and their sellers, ignoring their loose talk and crude banter, and stepped on to the dusty white road.

When Dara arrived home, his wife Chinda was frying fish in a wok, yesterday's catfish leftovers with some steamed rice. Without a word to his wife, the old policeman sat on a bench in the backyard under a banyan, swallowing the mashed fish bones and rice. His two dogs came out, staring at his food and waiting, but eventually even they got bored and started to chase each other in the yard. The sun was burning hot above Dara's head and flies whirled around his sweaty skin.

He had bought some gasoline from a roadside store, and filled the oil tank of his old Yamaha. For some days now, the engine of his disintegrating steel horse wouldn't start, and the sparks weren't jumping. Dara had been riding his Yamaha for nearly ten years, but now he had to fix the rotten thing twice a week. With the dogs fighting for their lunch nearby, he pulled the spark plug out and moistened the hole with a bit of gasoline, then he screwed in the spark plug and kicked at the bike to start it. Immediately, a puff of black smoke rose up and nearly set the motorbike on fire. The engine was working, and now the only parts that still needed to be fixed were the brakes, but Dara didn't care much. Who needed brakes? Brakes wouldn't get him to a village fifteen miles away in one short afternoon. All he needed was speed. Dara cooled down his face with a splash of water and jumped on his motorbike.

As the traffic gradually subsided, the old policeman's motorbike flew faster and faster along road to the jungle village of Khna. He descended south towards Lacustrine Plain, and his wheels gradually sank into water. The monsoon rain had been falling for weeks now, and the forest had become soaked in the afternoon's downpour.

Now, with the sun setting fire to his skin, thoughts of his lost daughter filled his mind. Normally Dara didn't think much; he only lived. But when he occasionally thought of his little daughter Bopah, big oily tears would roll quietly down his dark cheeks.

Dara was an orphan, and since he was a child there had been no one to count on or to care for. He had been wandering around the world like a weightless leaf. The day his wife bore him a daughter, he felt that he had finally become a true man and he wanted to love the little child for his next three lives. But then, Buddha and Angkor together had played their joke on his life. One day, when his daughter Bopah was four years old, she had been walking behind him on the way back home. As they passed a rice field, Bopah played with a white buffalo while Dara had a short chat with the rice farmer. At one point Dara realised he couldn't hear his daughter's laughter anymore. He turned around: the white buffalo was still there but Bopah was no longer playing on the grass. He searched around all the fields until the sky grew dark and the hairs on his skin stood straight. He walked to the nearby villages but again found nothing. He hoped that the girl had managed to get back home by herself, or that someone had helped her. He returned home, only to find his wife alone. Chinda began to cry bitterly. At night, the couple lay and waited on their bed, which was little more than a floorboard. Then his wife got up and lit a candle to pray to the Buddha all night. When the rooster sang at the break of dawn, Dara left the house and went back to the area around the rice fields. He searched the nearby jungle for days, but found no trace of his daughter.

Fifteen years passed, and the old policeman's wife had another two pregnancies but both of the babies died at birth. The midwife from the village said that Chinda had a very small womb; that it suffocated the child inside. The doctor from Siem Reap warned that if Dara's wife had another pregnancy, she would die. But the worst remark came from a witch in a nearby village. The witch told Dara that he had caught an evil spirit in his early life and that the bad spirit was resting in their house. She said that it would always accompany the policeman wherever he went. An evil spirit from his early life? The old policeman didn't ask what it was and neither did his wife. But after the witch had gone, his wife said, 'Perhaps that woman meant those people you killed years ago.'

When he heard this, the old policeman's head began to ache. He knew what the witch had been talking about, even if the witch herself did not. He was eighteen when the Khmer Rouge killings took place. He had been one of those 'New People', a young soldier of Pol Pot in the 70s. As an orphan he'd had neither education nor a home but in the army he found himself some rice to eat and a place to sleep. When the civil war broke out he was serving as a guard in a labour camp in the north. He had never met Brother Number 1 but nonetheless he was loyal to the leader's words. He had beaten many enemies and killed many people. He had dug big pits with other soldiers in order to bury the corpses. After the war, he had wandered through remote areas. For a few months, he went to Thailand to start a small business selling gasoline, but trade faltered. So he switched to recycling plastic bottles, refilling them with tap water to sell at the market. Back in the country, he spent his days riding a cyclo for the visitors touring the ancient Angkor temples. Life was about earning every day's rice – it had never let him look back. Eventually, since he was very good with guns and could shoot a target precisely, he got a job in the local police office. After living alone and being lonely for thirty years, Dara felt like settling down. He found himself a wife who came from a village near Tonlé Sap lake. Chinda was a simple woman who had never left her village before. But their happy life was finished even before it started. Their missing daughter became a sorrowful presence in their house, and when she learned she could no longer have babies, Chinda fell into a silent depression.

Months and years went by, and no one asked the policeman anything about his past. Perhaps once or twice his wife stared at him and wanted to know of the things that had happened thirty years ago, but even she gave up in the end. What would be the use? Everyone had suffered the civil war; every heart was dead many times over. His past was like a long night with a string of senseless nightmares. There was no energy left to talk about those bitter years. To survive was the only meaningful thing to do.

Then only yesterday, in the police office, Dara heard that an old woman had found a jungle girl in the forest. He learned that the jungle girl couldn't speak any human words and that she behaved wildly, like a feral beast. The villagers guessed that the girl had lived in the jungle for most of her life and therefore couldn't understand humans. But the second Dara heard that the jungle girl had a big purple scar on her left arm, he knew it was his daughter Bopah. Thoughts crowded the policeman's mind; thoughts that constantly tortured him and wouldn't leave him in peace. Dara convinced himself that his missing daughter was found. He didn't want to tell his wife yet.

After an hour with the wind cutting under a poisonous sun, thinking over the past and of his lost little daughter, Dara's cheeks were wet from his thick tears. Life was like a well dug long ago – you hoped the water supply would last the rest of your life but as the days went by, the well got drier and drier. Eventually, it became a deep and hollow dark hole. There were a very few things one could keep in this life, Dara thought. If an old man could manage to get something back from his past, then his future would still be worth living. Murmuring to himself, the old policeman drove over miles and miles of bumpy red dirt road alongside the banana trees.

Upon arriving in the village of Khna, Dara tried to find the family who had found the jungle girl. He got the name and a rough address from his office, and had bought a map as well. The area was poor, like the village where the old policeman had grown up. It had only a few mango and palm trees, and several buffalo. The locals made their living producing palm tree sugar – they would chop the tree trunk and heat the inside, letting the palm tree juice flow out, then they would dry the juice to make sugar. But Dara knew that palm tree sugar earned them very little money and that these people had to kneel by the fire all day long, under a hot sun, heating those tree trunks. There were no rice fields nearby and the land was occupied by shapeless bushes, grown after all the mahogany trees had been felled for furniture. The monsoon season had begun to show its power and most of the land was swallowed by a muddy, yellow water.

After a while, Dara found the grandmother who had discovered the jungle girl. The yard was full of barking dogs, chickens, cats and pigs, rats and lizards, and naked children. At first, the grandmother didn't want to show the jungle girl to the policeman, talking instead for about an hour. Holding her two grandchildren in both arms, she told Dara that for days, the food in her house had gone missing. Normally she would pack the food into two lunch boxes for her son and grandson, who worked as guards in the nearby temple. Since the food kept going missing, she decided to look around and find the thief. So she went into the jungle, which was further than the villagers would usually go. That was when she saw a naked girl with mud all over her skin, her long hair covering her body. The little beast was discovered kneeling down in the dirt, grabbing at rice and pork spread out on a huge banana leaf. The grandmother recognised the food and ran fast to catch the jungle thief. But to her surprise, the jungle girl didn't walk like a human. Instead, she ran on four limbs like a monkey. Yet even the grandmother was faster than the hunched monkey girl, and eventually she caught her and brought her back to the village.

When the old policeman saw the feral girl in the grandmother's backyard, his cheeks began to ache and his heart shrank. The jungle girl was lying under a dead banana tree, her body wrapped in a piece of cloth and her hands and feet tied by ropes to the tree. Her long hair covered her entire body like a black robe. Her eyes were the most frightened eyes Dara had ever seen, full of a certain hatred he couldn't understand. She didn't seem to care when flies and insects stuck to her skin. Dara looked carefully at the girl's left arm. Yes, some purple marks, just like he remembered on his little daughter.

When Dara moved closer to her, the jungle girl started to scream like an owl. He called his daughter's name, 'Bopah, Bopah!' but she trembled like a monkey caught in a forest fire. When Dara tried to untie her, the jungle girl became like a wild bull, biting into the rope around her shoulder. The grandmother said that the feral girl had been making just this kind of noise all night, barking at anyone who passed in front of her. The old policeman paid some riels as compensation for the old woman's food, and half an hour later, the village kids watched as the policeman tried to fix the girl on to his motorbike; it seemed to take all the old man's energy to manage this at last.

Back home in Siem Reap, the old policeman's wife burst into tears when she saw the jungle girl. She immediately prayed to the Buddah and then she seemed suddenly to become a woman of strength. Together, with great effort, the couple tried to give Bopah a bath, though the effort it required exhausted them. After washing her, Dara's wife attempted to dress the girl in a shirt, but as soon as the clothes were on, the feral child would violently tear them off again. Outside, the moon was already high in the sky; the night seemed to have arrived faster than any other night. Dara made some lentils but the food was left untouched – instead the wild one ate a cluster of bananas. They organised a small room and bed for her, then they left her alone. Dara made sure the door and windows of her room were always closed in case the girl ran away.

No one really knew what was going on inside Dara's house. The neighbours knew only that on the second day after the jungle girl's arrival, she tried to run away, but the neighbours caught her and brought her back. Another time, two journalists came to visit and took some photos of her. Then a week later, the neighbours discovered their chickens were going missing. They traced the blood all the way to Dara's house, and through the window they saw the girl sitting on her bed, blood and feathers around her mouth and in her hair. The neighbours ran back to their yard scared, without a word.

As the days went by, the old policeman was barely seen on the streets of Siem Reap. The couple were busy in their house, trying to teach their daughter to walk on her feet, and to speak, and cooking for her. The girl preferred to huddle in the corner, staring at everything with her big, secret eyes. Her teeth were so tightly clenched that Dara could hear them grating. She had hidden herself, rolled up, like a big silent cat, creating a suspended tension which left the couple sleepless. Worst of all, she couldn't get used to the habit of peeing or shitting in the toilet, she would relieve herself anywhere on the floor, or outside in the yard.

For weeks, the jungle girl's words were incomprehensible. But once, when Dara was alone with her in the house, she said 'papa' and looked into his face. Dara's throat tightened suddenly as he felt tears come into his eyes. Sometimes, in the middle of the night, when the mosquitoes were calming down, Dara's heart squeezed as he contemplated his daughter sleeping on the bed, like a dog would sleep – four limbs laid out vulnerably, head down inside her long thick hair. He wondered if there was any kind of memory stored in this wild girl's mind, the memory of what had happened to her in the jungle before she got to their house. Dara knew one could forget anything; he had forgotten most things from the days when he was a soldier in the Khmer Rouge camp. He didn't want to remember. He could almost see the fragments of his memory like a handful of dust thrown into the night sky, falling into a ruined forest where the world didn't offer any hope of forgiveness or redemption.

One day, two strangers arrived in Dara's front yard. One was an American, who wore a pair of elegant glasses and carried a silver suitcase; and the other was his assistant and translator, a Khmer living in Phnom Penh. The American said he was a psychologist and that he had read a newspaper article about Dara's jungle girl. This was why he had travelled all the way from the capital in a bus with his translator.

'What do you want?' Dara stared at the two men.

But it seemed that seven hours on the bumpy road had made the two civilised men unusually grumpy. The assistant asked for water and something to eat, while the

American went straight to the jungle girl's room. Dara's wife cooked some noodles and made icy lime-juice for them. Standing as close to his daughter as possible, Dara observed the foreigner touching the girl's hands and moving her arms, whilst at the same time speaking to her in English. It was bizarre for the old policeman to see – his own daughter couldn't even understand him and Chinda, so how would she understand a foreigner? But the American seemed to be very patient; he made crazy hand signs to the girl and took detailed notes in his notebook. All through this the poor little thing just stared at the foreigner with deep hatred in her eyes.

Eventually the American left her alone and tried to instruct Dara instead. The foreigner claimed that at the moment, the girl's intelligence was that of a four-year-old child and that because she had not been living with humans for so long, she would have to be systematically retrained from scratch. The psychologist explained that the girl needed to be treated in a special hospital in Phnom Penh, otherwise she wouldn't be able to live like a normal human. A special hospital in Phnom Penh. When the old policeman heard this, his face darkened. He could not imagine the girl being sent somewhere even further away than where he had at last found her.

As the American left the old policeman's house, he said to Dara, 'I also think it is necessary to do a DNA test on you and your . . . what's her name . . . Bopah.' It sounded like the psychologist didn't want to refer to the girl as Dara's daughter. But a DNA test? Dara knew what that was; he had worked as a policeman and he knew what it meant. Without saying anything, Dara smiled and sent the men to the front yard, then watched them disappear at the end of the road. Back inside, Dara locked the wooden barrier around his house, shutting himself, his wife and his daughter inside.

Dara was on his old Yamaha again. He had just left his district after completing a shift with another policeman and was now on his way to a temple in the outskirts of the city. He had heard that there was a spirit healer living in the temple who could help to exorcise the 'jungle spirits' from his daughter. He spent a good while there, negotiating the price with a monk. At last, they came to agree that Dara would pay thirty-five US dollars – the spiritual healer didn't want useless Cambodian currency. Dara's monthly salary was only thirty US dollars, but he was willing to pay anything to cure his daughter. Anyway, the monk explained, he would find out where the jungle spirits hid within the girl, and he would organise a ritual to get rid of them. Leaving the temple, Dara was full of hope and he rode his Yamaha back home as fast as he could.

The spirit healing was supposed to take place in the monk's temple, but Dara and his wife could not get their daughter out of the house – she refused to put on her clothes and she wouldn't walk on her feet. The next day, Dara had to pay another ten US dollars to invite the healing master to visit them instead.

The healing process was long and tedious; it took from dusk until dawn. Dara and Chinda were not allowed into the room, so they stayed in the yard under their three pathetic palm trees. Dara drank beer from the bottle, which fell and broke when he heard his daughter screaming in the house.

After the healing, the girl became quiet, or rather silent. She looked hurt, her huge, dark eyes hidden in her trimmed, short hair. Her head seemed heavy and loose on her shoulders. She was like a lion struck by the forest thunders, suddenly surrendering her wild temper to the lightning. Dara's wife kept her faith in the Buddha and continued to teach the girl to walk and to dress. Two days after the spirit healer left, the family was surprised to see that the girl could stand on her feet, and slowly, she began to walk around in the house. Her back was still hunched, like someone who had been living for a long time in a small cave. To Dara, it felt like the softest and saddest moment in his life.

In June, the monsoon rains flooded everybody's houses and Dara had to move everything upstairs. But compared with a month ago, the family felt calm. One morning, the rain stopped and the sun began to shine. To

Dara's surprise, the same American psychologist appeared again in front of his house, accompanied by a local doctor. Dara's wife greeted the two men once again with lime-juice. In a very direct manner, the local doctor suggested that he could take the whole family to a car, then drive them to the Phnom Penh hospital to do a DNA test, and after the DNA test, the psychologist said, he would be more than happy to assist further with the patient. The old policeman listened, finishing a whole bottle of Angkor beer before opening another.

For a while, the three men sat under the shade of the banyan tree in Dara's yard. The old policeman carried on drinking his beer, showing clearly that he wouldn't leave the house. With the help of the local doctor's translation, the American psychologist explained further what would work best in the case of the jungle girl, but once again, the American didn't use the word 'daughter'. Dara seemed not to be listening anymore; he just gazed at a green-skinned lizard lying underneath his rotten Yamaha in the sun. It didn't appear to move all afternoon. The American psychologist went back to the jungle girl's room, where he talked to her strangely and made his peculiar hand gestures. Eventually the sun sank towards the west, and the lizard also disappeared. The two men were about to leave but, once more, they asked if Dara would bring the girl and come with them. Dara shook his head.

Nothing else could be said. Now the old policeman and his wife accompanied the two doctors to their car, which was parked near the house. The doctors gave Dara their business cards, which Dara had already received on their first visit. Unsatisfied, they drove away. The old policeman stood still like a palm tree, watching the car disappear. He appeared thoughtful for a few minutes, as if he was making some difficult decisions. But in the end he shook his head, sat back under his banyan tree, and drank the rest of his beer.

The next morning, Dara and his wife were woken by a dog's loud barking. He got up and walked into Bopah's room – she wasn't there. Hastily he searched every corner of the house, including the back and the front yards, but his daughter was gone.

The search for the jungle girl went on for about two weeks. Nobody had seen her. The couple spent their days on the motor bike, searching up and down the streets of Siem Reap. When they left the city, they went down to the provinces, to those floating villages around the lake of Tonlé Sap, and then on to the mountains at the northern border. They rushed back to the area where the girl was first found and they stayed in the village of Khna for a while, but no one had seen a feral human being. Dara wandered in the jungles for days, amongst small monkeys and endless bushes, but he found no trace of the girl.

*

Time slipped away; as quietly as the white hair accumulating on the old policeman's head. The monsoon season was over – the streets and the roads became sandy and dry again, and the green papayas started to ripen and rot. Every day, as the old policeman drove his Yamaha up and down the street, he heard rumours about his jungle girl. Someone said that the last time they saw her, she was selling some finger bananas on a small road towards Angkor Wat, while others said they had seen her squatting on a boat in Tonlé Sap lake two months earlier. Some said they met her one night in front of a night club in Phnom Penh, and that she looked like a prostitute. Dara also heard that she had died in a traffic accident; that she hadn't stopped for the cars. But amongst all the talk, the most convincing story was that the jungle girl went back to the jungle. The jungle of the vast Lacustrine Plain, where the forest, the lake, the mountains and the rice fields had lain every century, every year and every day beneath the poisonous tropical sun.

After his wife died of lung disease, the old policeman lived the rest of his life in a temple in the north of the country. He still kept his Yamaha but he had returned his gun. Sometimes, as moonlit bats flew through the night, he tried to think of his past; to untangle those knots in his heart. He no longer wished for his past to be like a handful of weightless dust falling into a black hole. He wanted to keep it with him, every bit of it, like warm ashes resting in an incense burner before the old Buddha, each quiet, passing day.

Change

MARIE PHILLIPS

Marie Phillips was born in London in 1976. She studied anthropology and documentary making, and worked as a TV researcher and as an independent bookseller. Her first novel, *Gods Behaving Badly*, was published in 2007.

'So, did it change your life?'

We were sitting in a meeting room in one of the Plan International offices in Kampala, Uganda. I had stopped crying by then, but the four Plan workers were still looking at me with a mixture of concern and panic in case I started again. My face was sticky with the dust of a three-hour drive from Kamuli district, now distributed by tears into orange-red rivulets down my cheeks: attractive. But then probably also a good match for my sweaty clothes, mud-clogged Crocs, hair frizzed-up by rainy season humidity, dehydration-reduced physique, and general aura of exhaustion.

'Did it change your life?'

This was the only man in the room, a white American – perhaps Canadian. I hadn't taken in what he did for Plan, though he'd been there for years – perhaps decades – and was present for the debrief with The Writer (me) so I guessed it was something important. It seemed to matter to him, whether my life had been changed by visiting

Uganda, and it was just a shame that I didn't know the answer yet because I was still there and the only thing that had sunk in was the grime into my skin.

But I know now, in case he's still interested. And the answer is yes, yes it did. But probably not in the way that he had in mind.

It wasn't my first visit to Uganda. I'd actually been twelve years before, when my sister was living there, working for an environmental charity. So at first it seemed familiar. Arriving in the hot, crowded airport, the anxiety over what awaited me – or not – in the toilets (paper? soap? water? – one out of three ain't bad), the anxiety over whether my luggage awaited me at all and whether it would have everything in it that I had packed at the other end, the anxiety over whether the customs people would be feeling friendly or not and what they would make of my visa (visiting writers are never exactly embraced by third world immigration officials), anxiety over which of the jostling cab drivers was likely to have a functional vehicle and a non-fatalistic attitude to driving: anxiety, basically. And then bursting out into the wave of heat and noise, and my heart lifts, here I am, I'm in Uganda, and I'm probably not going to die on the way to my hotel. Probably . . .

Uganda is an unforgettably colourful place: bright red earth, lush dark green vegetation and a bold blue sky when it's not raining. The international airport is in Entebbe, about a half-hour drive from the capital Kampala, although it's hard to see where Entebbe ends and Kampala begins. The road between the two is lined all the way with shops, some no bigger than cupboards, painted the lurid colours of drinks company logos and emblazoned with slogans: 'Live on the Coke side of life!' 'Cadbury's tastes as chocolatey as it looks!' 'Africa's official drink of having a drink!' Mobile phone shops are everywhere – twelve years ago nobody had a mobile phone, but on this visit my phone would work better even in the most isolated villages than it does in most of the southern counties of England.

Also everywhere: people. On foot, on bikes and motorbikes, in cars, trucks and matatus, mini-van taxis covered in stickers swearing allegiance to Premiership football teams or Jesus (similar levels of fervour here) and stuffed insanely full of passengers. As a dignitary of sorts, however, I was being driven in a brand-new NGO pick-up truck, of which football and religious preferences were unknown. We spent most of our time in and around Kampala in gridlock. There had clearly been a population explosion since I was last there, but I felt encouraged: it's a population who can afford cars; it's a population who shop in all these eye-wateringly bright stores; it's a population, if the adverts on the pick-up's radio are anything to go by, who spend at least as much time trying to figure out the cheapest phone deal in bundles of texts and minutes as we do.

At the airport and the hotel, the people I met were lovely, friendly, open, and, as often as not, laughing. This is the joy of Uganda. On my previous trip, my sister took me to the Kampalan nightclub Ange Noir with a group of her Ugandan friends. Everyone was so relaxed that people cheerfully danced facing their own reflections in the mirrored walls, unafraid of embarrassment. I taught them the Macarena to great enthusiasm, and if they still dance the Macarena in Kampala it's thanks to me. ('Thanks' may be the wrong word to use here.) Uganda was the most welcoming place I had ever visited, and so far on this trip that welcome was as warm as ever.

But then the work of the trip began. On my last visit, we went to the Impenetrable Forest to track gorillas. First stop of this visit was the Moonlight Stars project, to meet a group of prostitutes. The first sign that as a tourist in Africa, no matter how frequently you visit, you're going to miss a lot of the 'real' Africa.

At Moonlight Stars – named after the sex workers' own term for themselves – we were led into a large tent pitched in front of a sexual health clinic, where a group of women in their early twenties were waiting for us. They sat on plastic garden chairs, their arms folded tightly in front of them. Their eyes were hard and they didn't smile. Everything about their body language was angry and untrusting. We were not welcome there.

This I had not expected. The Plan brochures I had been

sent, the images on the website and the brochures in the London office had all featured pictures of smiling children, grateful for what Plan calls its child-centred community development. 'Children are at the heart of everything we do,' says the Plan UK site. 'Children are our future. They carry our hopes and dreams for the world.' I had mentally put myself into those photographs with the happy kids, bringing them glad tidings from the West. Instead I was in a tent full of angry – and adult – prostitutes. If this was the reality of Africa, it was also the reality of NGO work.

Looking at my notes from that meeting, the first word I have written down is 'rape'. These women were raped before they became sex workers and they have carried on being raped ever since. One by one they told stories of being raped as teenagers, getting pregnant, being thrown out of home, and finding themselves unable to support themselves or their children. Enter a helpful friend who introduces them to the sex industry. 'Who looks after your children while you are out selling sex?' I asked. Answer: nobody. They leave them locked in their homes.

The streets of Kampala are not a safe place to sell sex. The women complained of rape from clients, rape from the police who periodically round them up to clean up the streets. Then there are the other risks, notably from HIV and AIDS. Condom use is not popular amongst johns in Uganda, and even if the prostitutes insist on it, it's easy to get around the issue by insisting on sex in a dark corner and then lying about the condom. And anyway, as one pointed out: 'You can get a man to use a condom but you are still a sex worker.' These are not happy hookers. The only time anybody laughed was when my Plan chaperone mentioned the Dutch model of legalised and regulated brothels, which reduced the entire group to hysterics.

The Moonlight Stars project aims to provide sex workers with healthcare – AIDS tests, condoms and so on – as well as training and financial support to help them set up their own businesses outside the sex industry, such as baking or hairdressing. But the funding has run out. So while Moonlight Stars *aims* to provide healthcare, financial support and training, what it actually provides is 'outreach'. I asked the women what outreach is. They told me that it's going out and telling other prostitutes about what Moonlight Stars *aims* to provide. Its not my last encounter with 'outreach' in Uganda. This is probably the right place to mention: outreach is cheap.

Before we left, the women asked us to give them money for the project. We explained that it doesn't work that way, that we have to report back to Plan in London who make the funding decisions. They were not impressed. In my notes I have written: 'I felt as if they were thinking: who the fuck are you and what are you here for if you're not going to give us any money?'

That night, my Plan chaperone and I ate our dinner in the hotel dining room while at the other tables, much older men sat with beautiful young women who were absolutely, definitely just there for the conversation. On the stage at the front of the room, a girl sang the Tracy Chapman song 'Fast Car'. 'You've got a fast car, I've got a plan to get us out of here . . .' A fast car isn't going to help much in Kampala. It's gridlocked.

The next day we did the three hour drive to the Kamuli district, where one of the communities Plan is working with is based. It was the kind of place I'd driven through on my last visit to Uganda, on my way to somewhere more interesting. An area 4,383 kilometres square with a population of 712,000, it is so devoid of interest to outsiders that it wasn't even in my guidebook to Uganda. Without ever giving it any proper consideration, I had somehow assumed that everywhere on earth is featured in a guidebook to somewhere or other, that there are no places that some intrepid tourists – the type who would deny actually being tourists – do not wish to visit. But of course the world is full of such places, places with no tourist 'attractions', with neither the landscape nor the culture to draw in holidaymakers, but just mile after mile of flat scrubby bush, built up with nondescript mud huts, divided by nondescript fields. This is where everybody else lives, the people who are not worth meeting in the places that are not worth photographing. This is the real lonely planet.

Aside from the roadside toilets, of which the less said

the better – just imagine – actually don't – the drive up was as bland as a Ugandan biscuit, and left me feeling similarly as if I'd eaten a mouthful of dust. (Ugandan biscuits are a travesty of the word, and when I handed out some all-butter shortbread I'd brought from home, the locals could not believe how delicious it was.) At one point, though, we passed an enormous billboard with the photograph of an African man in late middle age. 'You wouldn't let this man . . .' begins the slogan, but at first it was obscured by a tree. I tried to fill in the blank. Sell you a used car? Run your country? We passed the tree. 'You wouldn't let this man go with your teenage daughter, so why do you go with his? Cross-generational sex stops with you.' As we drove past I amused myself briefly thinking about what that poor man might have done to deserve being the least welcome daughter-shagger in Uganda. What I didn't realise was that this was the first and last attempt I would see to address older males' sexual behaviour in a region where the sexual pathology was about to be painfully revealed to me.

I didn't notice our arrival in Kamuli. The word 'community' had led me to expect some kind of recognisable village, with edges, and a centre, a Ugandan version of an English village green. But to my eyes it was just a sprawl, with no way of distinguishing it from anywhere else we'd passed. How did anybody know where the community started and stopped? Did everybody here know each other, or did they just get on with their lives more or less in isolation, like we do at home? The Plan workers I'd met in London had told me that the community got together with Plan and set their development priorities together, but I couldn't see how or where that would happen. It certainly couldn't be the way I'd pictured it: everyone turning up one morning to talk things over under a tree. There are thousands of people in this community: it would have to be a pretty big tree.

Our first stop in Kamuli was the Plan regional office, where we met the local team, all Ugandans, who greeted me with warmth, enthusiasm, and a total lack of knowledge of who I was and what I was doing there. Word had reached them that a visitor was coming from Plan UK to be shown around the Kamuli project, but not who or why. There were too many levels of communication between Plan in the UK and Plan here, and everything had got distorted along the way. I hoped that this didn't happen when they had something to discuss which actually mattered.

Over the coming days, I would learn that although the Plan Kamuli team live locally, most of them have left spouses and children behind to be there, and may see their family only every few weeks or even less often. They work long, demanding hours, with time off barely delineated as local people will come to them with their needs day and night, seven days a week. But the head of the team welcomed us into his office with huge smiles, and waved the latest addition to his workload: a letter from a local school of 1,250 children, all of whose latrines have collapsed under recent heavy rains. Can Plan help?

Apparently this wasn't a decision which could be made by Plan Kamuli, and would have to be referred upward. I looked at the letter. 'All the latrines' meant, in fact, five latrines. The headmaster was hoping for a grant to build eight new ones – one for every 157 children, rather than one for every 250.

From here I was taken to visit one of the other local primary schools – this one with functioning latrines at least – to witness some sex education training that was going on there.

Uganda, supposedly, has universal free primary education. In practice, even at the free schools parents are required to pay for uniforms, textbooks and meals, and anyway, most of the parents I met on my trip told me that the government-funded free schools are so poorly resourced that only the most desperate would consider sending their children there. By poorly resourced, what they mean is: few or no classrooms, desks, chairs, or books, and only the sporadic presence of teachers. At every school we visited there was an attendance chart on the wall of the head's office, registering not pupils' attendance, but teachers'. The wages are so bad that as often as not the teachers can't be bothered to turn up.

There's little risk of losing their jobs, because there's such a shortage of people willing or able to teach.

Primary schools in Uganda are typically attended by children between the ages of seven and fourteen, but schooling will be interrupted or terminated if parents can't afford to pay the expenses involved, if they need their children to stay home and help in the fields, for illness, for menstruation, for pregnancy, and so on. Many children therefore do not finish primary school until they are older, if at all, and most will never go to secondary school.

The first thing I noticed at this particular school was a series of low blue and white signs stuck into the ground, of the type which you might expect to read 'Do Not Walk on the Grass.' These ones had the Plan logo on them alongside those of two other NGOs, and said things like: 'Virginity is Healthy for Boys and Girls', 'Young Children Say No to Gifts for Sex' and 'Sex Does Not Make Breasts Grow'.

The training itself was going on in one of the classrooms, where a mixed group of staff, parents and representatives of the student council had gathered. The discussion was already under way when I got there, so I slipped in, sat down next to a Plan employee and asked him what was happening.

'We are making girls aware of HIV and AIDS, so that they know the negative impact if male teachers make sexual advances.'

He didn't tell me the positive impact of male teachers making sexual advances.

The woman running the training session was rather more impressive. She was a large, commanding woman, exuding authority, and I was instantly terrified of her. If she had said jump, I would have not only checked how high, but what style of jump she preferred. Looking back on it, we were probably about the same age. Stuck on the walls behind her were lists of girls' roles and responsibilities in school and at home. At home, girls must cook and serve food, fetch water, clean the house, compound, clothes and cooking utensils, collect firewood and look after children and elderly relatives. I don't do all that, and I'm an adult. Then, at school, girls sweep the buildings, look after the grounds, fetch water, serve food and welcome guests. That's aside from their actual schoolwork, of course.

The room then started to discuss the attributes of a girl-friendly school. It became clear that one of the key concerns needing to be addressed was sexual abuse, and the moderator led us towards consideration of requirements such as female counsellors and private counselling rooms where girls can express their concerns, female teachers and senior girls acting as mentors, as well as more straightforward practical steps such as putting up fencing to protect girls from men on the outside. One of the fathers in the room kept interrupting to say that what girls really want is flowers, 'because girls are attracted to beauty', or attractive uniforms, 'because girls will like the school with the best-looking uniform'. The moderator acknowledged these interjections politely before returning to the point. It's important, she told me afterwards, that parents are part of the training sessions, and afterwards they are sent into the community to train other parents. It's a laudable aim, but with the fathers so unwilling to hear the darker implications of the discussion, it's hard to know how much impact these sessions can have.

After the session, the local Plan Child Protection Officer, who had been working nearby, hitched a lift with us back to her office, which is a hut in the centre of one of the Kamuli district villages. That she is enormously popular here was self-evident: every child that we passed smiled, waved and called out her name. There are hundreds of children in her area and she knows them each individually. That the Child Protection Officer would be on first-name terms with every single child of the region is both extraordinarily commendable and deeply upsetting.

The office walls were covered in posters, most of which are advice to children on how to avoid sexual abuse. As with the signs in the school, the key message is abstinence: 'I Always Say No to Sex' read one poster. I tried to imagine a campaign against child abuse in the UK choosing to focus so heavily on the child's responsibility to say no. But the CPO told me that it is necessary there.

Girls are so poor they will have sex in return for anything at all – for one chapati. Male schoolteachers are known to offer high grades in return for sex, and given the value of a good education here, many girls agree to it. I asked what happens if a male teacher is found to be having sex with his students. 'He is transferred to another school.'

But sexual abuse is not the only thing that children here are vulnerable to. The CPO told me about a case in which a thirteen-year-old girl was abandoned by her father after she developed epilepsy. He locked her out of the house and refused to give her any food, making her sleep outside, alone, in the rainy season, for three months. With Plan's support the father was arrested and successfully prosecuted, and the girl now lives with her mother. There are an overwhelming number of cases, the CPO said, and not enough resources to help them all. But she does her best, with the help of volunteers from the community.

Later I asked one of these community volunteers what has improved since Plan came to the area. 'Child protection,' he said without hesitation. What else, I asked. This time he had to think for a bit. 'Nothing,' he said.

I found out more about the 'negative impact' of HIV and AIDS the next day in a visit to a local hospital. The hospital comprises several buildings scattered around a compound, but only has one full-time doctor, plus a volunteer doctor and a number of midwives. This isn't too bad, considering that country-wide there is only one doctor for every 23,000 Ugandans. I kept having to remind myself, looking at the patients sitting or lying on the dirty concrete floor, with no food or water, waiting for hours to be seen, that these people are lucky. There was one old woman lying on the ground, immobile, with only a thin cotton wrap between her and the hard floor. Right at that moment, as it happened, my own grandmother was in a hospital in France. A few days later, in fact, she would die, but to the last she would be in a comfortable bed, with clean sheets and blankets, and 24-hour medical care. I imagined her lying in front of me, on that floor. I am still imagining that.

The hospital workers I met were determined and positive about recent improvements in HIV and AIDS care. All pregnant women who come to the hospital are counselled about HIV/AIDS, and those who consent are tested. People are now also coming forward for voluntary testing, I was told – this is new, and reflects the decreasing stigma of the disease, and the growing understanding that treatment can help extend life expectancy. There has also been an increase in the number of people seeking treatment, and staying in treatment programmes. I was told that if a pregnant woman follows the whole of the PMCT (Prevention of Mother to Child Transmission) programme, it will successfully prevent transmission of HIV to their baby in all cases. Unfortunately, it is rare that any of the women here can successfully complete the programme, as one of the key preventative factors is not to breastfeed your baby, but the cost of formula is $9 a week, and the average Ugandan income is less than a dollar a day.

When I asked the hospital administrator where the funding comes for the hospital, he laughed and reeled off a seemingly endless stream of NGOs, as well as the local health authority. It's hard to imagine just how much time is taken up administering and coordinating all of these separate income sources. And with so many different organisations with different priorities funding different services in the same place, key areas of provision fall through the cracks. So, for example, Plan's most notable contribution to the hospital is a machine which counts CD4 cells for HIV/AIDS patients – an invaluable piece of equipment, without which it is impossible to decide which ARV drug to prescribe, and at what dose. People travel from miles around just to have their blood tested by the machine. We are taken to visit the machine. I basically have no idea what I am looking at. It looks like a machine. But everyone is clearly very proud of it. Unfortunately, the machine needs specific reagents to make it work, and Plan don't provide these, and neither does anybody else. Supplies of the reagent can come from local government, but are as often as not stolen, both before and after they reach the hospital – drug theft is a huge crime here, as the resale value is immense. So, much of the time, when patients come in to have their blood tested, the trip is wasted. And anyway, chances are that even if the CD4 machine is working, the ARVs will have run out, for the same reason – lack of funding, and fraud. But the theory of PMCT is very good.

Waiting for us outside under a tree were members of the PMCT group, all HIV positive themselves, who do outreach in the community. They had been waiting for hours, because we were running late. In fact we were two hours late leaving Kampala on the first day because of petrol shortages in the city, and we would be late for every single appointment from then on, and yet people would wait for us, sometimes for hours, and we never heard a solitary complaint about it.

As soon as they saw us coming, the PMCT group leapt to their feet and began singing and dancing. We thought it was just a welcome – the welcomes there are terrifyingly elaborate, often involving ululations, and it does feel slightly lame to then extend your hand and say 'How do you do.' But in fact they were singing for us some of the songs that they use to explain issues around HIV and AIDS to people in the surrounding villages. My Plan chaperone – like me, a visitor from England – danced along to the songs, but I didn't, because I was too embarrassed, and then I was ashamed of being embarrassed, and then I was embarrassed of being ashamed, and all remaining hope of me dancing drifted away on a zephyr of British reserve.

The songs and dances are impressive, and an effective way of spreading the word, because in a village where there is no other form of entertainment, if a group of strangers turn up and start singing and dancing, you are going to go and have a look. They travel a long way to spread their message, up to 60km to some of the most remote villages, but although Plan have provided some bicycles for them, they need more. They also need money for musical instruments, for costumes for the short dramas they perform, and so on. As with the clinic, funding is piecemeal and comes from multiple sources. The group has been encouraged to raise their own money by making handicrafts, such as beads, baskets and mats, but there isn't anybody around who wants to buy these things. The idea is to sell to tourists, but there are no tourists here. There are just other impoverished Ugandans who don't give a toss about beads.

More disturbing was what the group told us about the home visits they make to AIDS sufferers who are too sick to visit the hospital. The project is so poorly funded that they can't even afford plastic gloves or basins, which makes it dangerous to touch and wash the wounds of patients, whose AIDS-related illnesses often leave them covered in lesions and sores. Their families are too afraid to touch them, and the patients too weak to look after themselves, so the wounds fester. Many afflicted families will own only one bucket, which they have to use for everything, from washing themselves, to washing food and dishes, to vomiting into. Families also can't afford separate bedding, which means that they sleep all together, so even where AIDS is not transmitted, AIDS-related illnesses, such as TB, are.

The next day I was taken to visit another school, one of the most deprived in the area. Why I'd come, and what was Plan's involvement with the school, was not clear. But in any case, I was shown around. Almost two hundred of the youngest children were squeezed into the same classroom, which was also used for storing firewood. The headmistress' office had also been divided into two so that half of it could be used as a classroom for the older kids. The buildings had pockmarked walls, heaped earth instead of floors, and holes for windows. Still, those that have classrooms at all are lucky, as many of the children have to learn sitting on the ground outside. On the day that I visited, the thought of having lessons out of doors in the sunshine seemed idyllic. It is probably less pleasant during the monsoon, when the dust beneath our feet turns to several inches of mud.

We'd been told that there was going to be an assembly, but what I hadn't realised was that I was expected to give it. I was seated at a desk while all of the girls gathered under a tree, sat cross-legged on the ground and stared at me. I stared back. If I hadn't known that they were girls I would not have been able to tell. School-age children in Uganda wear their heads shaved, and the girls were so poorly fed that they didn't have hips or breasts. They had the sexless look of pre-pubescent children; I couldn't even tell how old they were. I said hello, how are you, which seemed like a good place to start. 'We are humble and obedient', they chorused in perfect unison. Bloody hell. I tried to imagine this happening in a British school, failed, and would have got the giggles were it not for the terror that any moment I was going to have to say something to these children, say quite a lot of things, and I was completely unprepared. I was, however, reassured that a few of them looked neither humble nor obedient, especially those at the back. They were still children, after all.

My Plan chaperone spotted my discomfort – possibly from the way I glared at her, eyes wide with panic, mouthing HELP – and suggested that the girls separate into small groups and discuss the topic of what they did and didn't like about school, choosing one girl from each group to present their findings. It was a brilliant idea and I wanted to kiss my Plan chaperone for sparing me from having to address a field full of Ugandan children on What It Is Like Being a Freelance Author in London – a topic which would have come as a particular surprise to the schoolteachers, to whom I had been introduced, bafflingly, as a 'consultant'.

The girls were separated into groups and talked quietly amongst themselves as I enjoyed the shade of the tree and tried not to let my stomach rumble. We were so busy in Kamuli, and inevitably running so late, that for the entire time we were there we never found time to eat any lunch. It was hard to feel any self-pity about this, as many of the people we met there ate only once a day, and twice seemed about average.

The teacher called the girls to attention and asked each group to present the findings from their discussions. The spokespeople for the first four groups all answered the question 'What do you like about school?' by saying what they hoped to achieve by going to school – the jobs that they hoped to get. Either they liked school so little that they could only see it as a means to an end, or they were so delighted to have the opportunity to go to school and the chance to improve their lot in life that it outweighed all else. Indeed the two are not mutually incompatible. Anyhow, two of the girls voiced fairly predictable aspirations: to be teachers or doctors or nurses. Everywhere I went in Uganda and asked children what they want from life, this is what they answered. I wonder what they would make of surveys in the UK where girls consistently report that when they grow up they want to be 'famous'. The other two girls had loftier dreams, though: one said that she wanted to be a pilot, and the other that she hoped to be President of Uganda. The entire group whooped, clapped and cheered at her audacity, and maybe it's not such a wild hope: the current deputy speaker of the Ugandan Parliament is a woman from this very area, who grew up in exactly the poverty I was witnessing.

When asked what they didn't like about school, each of the girls spoke about the problem of menstruation. Although it's stating, as it were, the bloody obvious, its worth remembering that on average girls have their period for one week in four, and in a country where many girls can't afford underwear and almost none can pay for sanitary protection, this is hugely debilitating. The girls told us that they use banana fibres (apparently fairly effective) or plastic bags (rather less so), as sanitary protection, but that the school doesn't have adequate toilet facilities to allow them to change their protection or clean themselves up. They don't even have any toilet paper. I tried to imagine dealing with my period with only plastic bags and no toilet paper, and, as so many times on this trip, failed. It's no wonder that many girls do not attend school while they're menstruating. Would you?

By the time the fourth girl was complaining about the difficulty of dealing with periods while at school, the head teacher was clearly embarrassed and interrupted to say that these distinguished visitors from England really didn't want to sit around all afternoon hearing about menstruation, and could they please come up with something else?

So the girl who was speaking stopped, gave it some

thought, and then said that some girls are mistreated by their stepmothers, who withhold their basic needs, such as food and soap, so they have sex with boys in order to meet those needs, and then they become pregnant and have to leave school.

The ban on talking about menstruation opened a floodgate of terrifying revelations about what it is like to be a Ugandan schoolgirl, all delivered in a matter-of-fact tone and received with no surprise by the other girls or the teachers. This, lest we forget, is what is considered by these girls to be the second worst thing about school, after periods. I wrote everything down as fast as I could in my notebook, trying to capture it all. When I read back over it later, I could barely believe my eyes. *(6)*, I had written. *Good: can become professional — doctor, nurse, teacher. Bad: boys disturb them because they are girls, take them into the bush and make them pregnant. Stepmothers don't give them food. (7) Good: learn singing, athletics, sport. Bad: very vulnerable to men on way to school. Men grab and rape them. (8) Problem of child marriages. Parents force them into early marriage and they have to leave school. Likes: art and crafts. (9) Admires teachers and studies hard to be like them. Talks about other problem of being raped: ie catching HIV and AIDS.*

The *other* problem of being raped?

On the last day, we finally visited the school which had no latrines. They still had no latrines, though there was a solitary man with a spade, digging a ditch for a temporary replacement. It had been six days since we arrived in Kamuli district and read the headmaster's letter. Meanwhile the school had only been open for half days so that the students could go home and use the latrines there.

Or at least most of the students could. What I hadn't realised was that this school, as many in the region do, takes boarders. It's the only solution for families who live more than two hours' walk from a school. Less than two hours' walk is considered to be fine. That's two hours each way, usually in the dark – not at all unusual for a Ugandan child. It is on these walks that girls are most vulnerable to rape, and so there's a direct correlation between poverty and rape – the poorest children tend to be from the most isolated villages, living the furthest from the schools, and walking the longest distances to get there.

Once we had examined the collapsed latrines (I didn't examine them very closely), the Head showed me the girls' dormitory. Eighty-six girls share one room, only half of whom have beds. The others sleep on the floor. The ground is so crowded with bedding that you can barely get into the room, which is stultifyingly hot, even though there is no glass on the windows. No glass, and no mosquito netting. Malaria is the leading cause of death in Uganda and there wasn't a single mosquito net in this room. Not only are they sleeping on the floor of a barn which smells like the Elephant House at London Zoo, not only do they not have a hole to shit in, but these girls don't even have the most basic bit of fabric which might just get between them and death from malaria. One mosquito net costs 50p. Mosquito nets for every girl in this room would cost £43.

Our work in Kamuli completed, it was another three-hour drive back to Kampala and we gave a couple of the Plan workers a lift so that they could visit their families. There were five of us crammed into the truck, and as one of the women was eight months pregnant it was a bit of an anxious ride, particularly as for the first hour there was no tarmac and the road was extremely bumpy. Once, when I was on a long-haul flight, the woman in the seat next to me went into labour, and afterwards I asked a doctor friend to tell me how to deliver a baby, just in case it ever happened again. It's not something I wanted to have to try out by a Ugandan roadside, although I did have some antibacterial hand gel in my bag.

We fell into conversation about a family we had just visited, a man with two wives and two daughters, one from each wife. The girls were part of a Plan cohort study that my chaperone was coordinating of 135 girls worldwide, from birth up to age nine, called 'Real Choices, Real Lives'. The theme for the 2009 report was Girls' Economic Independence. The girls in the cohort were two years old and didn't seem very economically independent to me, but then again, I'm not an academic. Anyway, at first the man had pretended that one of his wives was his sister because he was worried that otherwise the girls would not get into the study, and therefore they would miss out on the benefits of taking part. But there are no benefits, because that would be inequitable to the other people in the community, so it wasn't really worth the deception.

The Plan workers – both Ugandan, both married women – told me that polygamy is still common in Uganda. I thought back to what the girls in the school I visited told me about their stepmothers not giving them any food, and wondered what it would be like to be the child of the least favoured wife. I asked the Plan workers whether the arrival of a new wife is something that women find particularly welcome. Answer, not very surprisingly: no, but they don't have any choice. I asked whether women ever take a second husband, and the Plan women descended into fits of laughter. Then one of them said that if a man is unfaithful, it makes his wife very sad, but she learns to live with it. I asked what happens if a woman is unfaithful. 'Her husband will kill her,' she replied. I assumed that this was just an expression, like *If you leave the milk out again I'm going to kill you,* until she went on to talk about the problem of domestic violence in Uganda. There is no specific law against domestic violence in Uganda, and even where a woman does report an assault it is generally dismissed as being a private matter, to be resolved between the couple at home. Surveys consistently show that around 70% of Ugandan women have experienced domestic violence, but I was not brave enough to ask the two women in the car if they ever had. Anyway, they had gone back to giggling and imagining how their men would react if they got home and announced they were taking another husband.

Coming back to Kampala after my time in Kamuli felt like coming home. Despite the noise and the dirt, the bustle of the big city was reassuring, all the activity suggesting that these people's lives were going somewhere, that these people, at least, had hope. I thought that the worst of my trip was over, now that I was back somewhere familiar. After we'd dropped our passengers off we drove to Plan Uganda's headquarters in a smart suburb of Kampala, to debrief our visit. Every single building along this road appeared to house an NGO. According to DFID there are well over 2,500 NGOs operating in Uganda, which is about one for every 10,000 people. Or to put it another way, there are almost three times as many NGOs as there are doctors.

My chaperone and I were greeted warmly and shown to a meeting room upstairs where the head of Plan Uganda and two senior employees were waiting for us. We had a lot to talk about, and many questions to ask. My chaperone had only been with Plan for a few months and had never been to Uganda before, so everything we'd seen had been as new to her as it was to me.

We began our debrief, taking turns to tell about the people we had met and the deprivation we had seen. We had our own areas of interest: I had been most horrified by the schools, while she had been chiefly appalled by the clinics.

But – 'Did they ask you for money?' interrupted the American (or Canadian) man.

Well, yes. The schoolteachers showed us the over-crowded, falling-down school buildings, the lack of desks and books, and asked us for money. The people in the clinics told us of the huge demand for their services, and the lack of medicine and equipment, and asked us for money. The families we visited greeted us with politeness, offered us drinks, answered our questions, sometimes for several hours, and then, when we asked if there was anything we could do for them, asked us for money. Everybody asked us for money. This was understandable. We had money and they didn't. Moreover, we were representing the NGO who are working in the area with the stated aim of helping them. Of course they were going to ask us for money. We didn't give them any, but I didn't object to being asked. Had the roles been reversed, I would have asked them.

The American (or Canadian) shook his head. 'They always ask for money,' he said. 'They ask us for everything.' He said that there's a problem with a culture of dependency. You can't just give people what they ask for, or they'll never stop asking.

What this meant in practice was: no buckets for the AIDS workers, no reagents for the CD4 machine, and no latrines for the school. None of the things that we'd seen were going to get done.

What about the sexual abuse, I said. Everywhere we went, there were signs and posters and projects to teach girls to say no to sex. But very little seemed to be being done with the men, to stop them from abusing the girls.

'There is a culture of submissiveness amongst Ugandan women,' said the American (or Canadian). 'It's not as if anybody is holding a knife to their throats.'

This is the point at which I started to cry. I don't know what I said exactly, but between sobs and snot and mouthfuls of spit, I managed to get something out along the lines of: How dare you. How dare you suggest that these girls are to blame for getting raped. How dare you bring me over here and show me all of this need and then tell me that you can't help these people. I am just an author from London, an author of lightweight novels, I do not know anything about the culture of dependency or the culture of submissiveness, all I know is that I have met these people and they are poor and they are desperate and they are being raped, and they asked me to help them and I said that I would, and now you are telling me that you can't help them because of the culture of this and that, but what you can do is fund a cohort study into the economic independence of two-year-old girls, and what you can do is pay for an author to come over from London to write a piece for an anthology which will make people think that if they donate money it will go to the people that she met and the problems that she wrote about, only it's not going to go to them because of the culture of bullshit, so where the fuck is it going to go?

'What do you want?' said the head of Plan Uganda.

I just want those kids in that school to have a toilet.

'We will build them a toilet. You can come back and have your photograph taken with it.'

This is when I stopped crying because I was so angry. But, I said, you said that you couldn't build it. Because of the culture of dependency. What about the culture of dependency? Doesn't the culture of dependency matter any more?

'We will build them a toilet,' the head of Plan Uganda reassured me, as if this answered my question. Which, in a way, it did.

And this is when the man said: 'So, did it change your life?'

And I said: 'I don't know.'

But I do know now. And my visit to Uganda totally changed my life. I discovered that I have more power in the nib of my pen than 1,250 Ugandan children with no toilet. And I discovered that, in order for anybody to hear you cry, you need to be rich and white and sitting in the right office. But in the end, who cares whether this visit changed my life. The real question is, did it — will it — change their lives, the people of Kamuli?

A Response

SUBHADRA BELBASE, COUNTRY DIRECTOR OF PLAN UGANDA

Subhadra Belbase has worked as a journalist and for several NGOs in her native Nepal and in Bangladesh, Egypt and Sri Lanka. She worked for Plan for eleven years from 1989–2000 and re-joined in 2008 after working for a small NGO in Nepal for 7 years. She is currently Country Director for Plan in Uganda. She is the author of a collection of short stories, *Mero Nepal* (My Nepal), published in 2008. Her stories are concerned with women's lives and with the struggle and hope for change.

'Had I not on several occasions, spent sleepless nights after witnessing horrific poverty or injustices?' I asked myself. Author Marie Phillips had just returned from the Nawansaso Primary School in an area yet to benefit from Plan's work. She had witnessed how girls at the school sleep on the floor. It had an understandably and visibly profound effect on Marie.

'Guilt,' I thought, 'We all seem to go through the same stages.' Flashes of my own first experience of intense guilt for my 'privileged life' passed through my mind, as I put my arms around a sobbing Marie. She is as young as my own son, and I felt protective of her.

'What do YOU want to do?' I asked Marie, I empathised with her.

'I want to raise money for the school and make sure the girls have a decent dormitory and toilets,' Marie responded.

I visualised another school, the Kamuli Girls' School – one not visited by Marie. The well-maintained school, built with community support and with funds raised by Plan now has clean toilets, a modern kitchen, a large auditorium, borehole, income-generating projects and soon the girls will be getting a new dormitory. The confident girls at this school lead their area in two key campaigns 'Because I Am a Girl' and 'Learn without Fear', both of which focus on the rights of young women like them to a decent education and to real opportunity.

'OK, then. If you raise the money specifically for the dormitory and toilets, we will use the money for just that. And when the toilets are ready, you can come here and have a photograph taken in front of the school,' I said, imagining the smiles on the faces of the children who would use the new toilets with funds raised by Marie Phillips.

But money alone will not fix anything. We had obviously failed in explaining to Marie the child-centred rights-based approach to development where, to quote President Obama's now famous 'African speech', 'we are partners in bringing transformational change. Aid is not an end in itself. The purpose of foreign assistance must be in creating the conditions where it is no longer needed.'

Plan works towards this goal by focusing on activities that are best for the children. We go through a rigorous five-to six-month planning process with the people living in the communities. All family members – children, women and men – local government officials, schoolteachers and any other community members spend weeks discussing the problems and how we can resolve them. Based on this we come up with an action plan, which lists the activities that must be implemented in the next five to six years. Usually the list of things to do is very long. We have a rough estimate of the funds Plan might raise for Uganda. Based on this estimate we decide on activities the members of the parish/school/government will do and others that Plan can support them to implement.

For example, while conducting a planning exercise, some community members told Plan that the health clinics that we had constructed did not have malaria tablets and requested Plan to purchase these. Plan staff stood firm. The government must stock its clinics with malaria tablets. I had followed up this issue with the State Minister for Health. 'Plan should never supply malaria tablets to the district,' he told me, 'because we send money for tablets, or stocks of malaria tablets to the districts. This means the district officials are pocketing the money!'

It is common knowledge amongst all development and social workers that if individuals contribute even nominal amounts for services or goods, then they take more responsibility for themselves and take good care of what they have paid for.

Based on this lesson learnt, Plan provided the district clinic with a Cell Differentiation Machine, the CD4 machine mentioned in Marie's story, which is used to detect the level of immunity for HIV and AIDS blood cells. Plan also provided the first instalment of the reagents, chemicals used by the CD4 machine to test the blood for HIV and AIDS needed to make it work. We trained medical staff on how to use the machine and fix it should it break down. Users are expected to pay 5,000 Ugandan Shillings for this service which costs 55,000 in private clinics. The collected fees are used to purchase the next batch of reagents. But like most other drugs in Uganda, reagents were not available when Marie visited the clinic. To date, Plan is subsidising the government clinic to purchase reagents because the 5,000 shillings paid by the people tested so far in Kamuli is insufficient. With the machine and reagents supplied by Plan, 800 people in Kamuli have tested their HIV and AIDS status. Those tested positive are on medication; with new purchases of reagents more people will be tested. We work in very difficult political and social environments and if we compare hospitals in the developed world with the developing world, we will definitely be shocked. We need to ask the question as Marie asks, 'Has Plan impacted the lives of the children and people we serve?' We definitely have. In this case 800 people now know whether or not they need treatment. More will follow. And we know for sure that getting people to test their status is the first most difficult hurdle to overcome when we work in HIV and AIDS.

*

A Response

I had come to Uganda in June 2008 to take over as Country Director of Plan. During the three-week handover, my predecessor and I had travelled to the four districts where Plan works. In Tororo district, I had been deeply impressed with one particular project. I understood that Plan had built on eight years of experience and lessons learnt on HIV and AIDS to design the pilot Prevention of Mother to Child Transmission. There were initially fifteen partners working on this project. The model that was developed is lauded all over the world. But it took us almost fifteen years to achieve such results and we have saved the lives of more than 3,000 people who suffer from AIDS. Plan is preparing to hand over this project to the government. That is what we aim at – to build the capacity of government to discharge their duty to the citizens of the community Plan works in.

In Tororo I had also admired the community in Mublua. The women's craft group export their handicrafts to Ireland. It takes patience, and several years of training, to enhance the rudimentary skills the women and men have to produce quality export goods, and find markets. This is the kind of independence Plan aims to achieve in all we do. For the purpose of aid, either government aid or NGO aid, is to create conditions where aid is no longer needed.

It is with pride that I can say that Plan has supported over two hundred schools in Uganda with building construction, boreholes, school furniture, textbooks, exercise books, and pencils, so that parents who cannot afford to purchase these materials can send their children to school. We also try to make sure that girls have their own toilets, because we know, as the girls have told us, that once they reach puberty they want privacy.

Like Marie, I too was upset that all messages on sexual violence were aimed at girls. But I understood the context: Ugandan schools, supported by Plan or not, were displaying messages approved by the President of Uganda, who was imitating the US President Bush's 'say no to sex' campaign.

I can easily relate to the social context in Uganda, because my frame of reference is my own country, Nepal, not the UK. So I empathise with the Ugandan women who, like the Nepali girls of my generation, are taught from childhood to be 'obedient and submissive'. Yet I am shocked by how Ugandan men take advantage of this submission and have several wives or children from several wives; shocked that some men abandon their families and feel no responsibility to the children they have fathered.

The Moonlight Stars, the group of sex workers who Marie describes in her write-up, receives Plan sponsored reproductive health services. These include information and training on HIV and AIDS prevention, training on how to educate peers, training materials, post-abortion care, tests for sexually transmitted diseases (STDs), contraceptives and counselling. They also spread the message on HIV and AIDS, and inform others like themselves where they can get health support. This is very important in the Ugandan context, because in most developing countries women do not know where to go for treatment, and have no information on how they can get infected with HIV.

The members of the Moonlight Stars and I talked woman to woman: 'How is it for women in your country?' they asked me.

'Well, we too are second-class citizens, but sexual abuse is not so prevalent, nor do men abandon their children as they do here. Our family system is much, much stronger.'

We laugh. Some smiles are sad.

'I wish our men were more like the men in your country!' says one girl.

I looked at the male Plan staff who accompanied me.

'That is true. Nepali men are far more responsible for their families.'

The men are not happy. Some male staff think that this female country director favours women. But I don't really care. I have heard this before from other men in other countries, including my own, and I know that my actions will bring some change. That is the most I can expect.

Given this context, perhaps it is not surprising that five months into my work, when I dropped into the office of one of Plan's technical advisers, a Ugandan man, to follow up on some work, he was horrified by this female intrusion.

'Why do you want to know?' he questioned.

'If I don't want to know who else will?' I asked, rather shocked. It soon dawned on me that this was the first time that Plan Uganda had a woman as Country Director.

'Not again!' I thought. Every assignment I have had in Plan, I have been the first woman to hold that position in that country. And over the years, I have learnt to take these firsts in my stride – as a challenge I must overcome so that I pave the way for other women. After a number of such encounters with this male, I asked some female staff, 'Why does X behave like this?'

'Oh!' they laughed, 'He belongs to Y tribe. The men in that area think they are definitely superior to women.'

'And you don't confront him?' I asked.

'Why create tension?' was the response.

I confronted Mr X. I told him how I felt. He was shocked. He had not realised that a woman found his behaviour unacceptable, and was even more amazed that she could tell him so!

And this self-realisation in him is the first step towards a possible change in his behaviour.

It is deplorable that we must live with this prejudice against women, and inevitably creates a bad impression on outsiders.

A Response

*

Marie's article brings up many other issues. 'Didn't you know that Marie is a writer?' I asked staff after reading Marie's write-up and her objection to the way she was introduced.

'Of course we did. All of us knew,' retorted Monica and Harriet who accompanied Marie Phillips and Dr Pauline Lane on their trip.

'I slipped once, while introducing Marie,' confessed Harriet, 'I called her a consultant. But does it really matter? All *musungus* (white people) are the same, especially to the community.' Will deprived, malnourished people be truly interested in the career differentiation of a people they have a blanket name for – *musungu*?

Recently, a year into my work in Uganda, I told Jim – the same Jim who asked Marie if the visit to Kamuli had made an impact on her – 'I am happy that some members of staff are opening up to me . . . the culture of silence is gently cracking . . .'

'Not with me – and I have been here four years,' Jim responded.

'Well, you are a *musungu*!' I teased.

Transparency International, in its 2008 report, has listed Uganda as the third most corrupt country in the world. The sequence of events leading to the suspension of the 201-million-dollar Global Fund to fight AIDS, Tuberculosis and

Malaria allocated to Uganda because of 'mismanagement' by its govenment is but one example among hundreds of similar cases. Donor funds provided to investigate this mismanagement also disappeared from the bank accounts. After this, newspapers reported that thugs vandalised the Directorate of Public Prosecutions which housed the financial records of the Global Funds!

Many international NGOs like Plan also discover corruption in some form within their own employees. After investigating one such misappropriation, I terminated the employment of a Program Manager.

The very next day, I was told by three Plan staff that this same manager had been sexually harassing female staff.

'But why were you quiet before?' I asked, deeply disturbed. I travelled around the four Plan district offices, talking to staff about our sexual harassment policy, the whistle-blowing policy, and what I thought was a 'culture of silence' in Plan Uganda.

'How can we teach communities about gender equity, if we do not practise it ourselves?' I asked.

I was still tossing and turning in bed, worrying about this culture of silence until, in June 2009, I was watching TV news. The results of a study on abuse of children by the church-affiliated schools in Ireland were being publicised. 'No one talked about it' wrote an Irish journalist in the *New York Times*. 'There was a culture of silence for decades.'

Female staff in Plan have developed a gender equity

training proposal for all Plan staff in Uganda. I am confident that within my remaining four-year term this training will bring about some change and that perhaps a few 'positive deviants' will courageously take the lead for other men and women to follow.

So, Marie, should you decide to raise funds for the girls' school in Kamuli, you will use the might of your pen to bring about some positive change for girls and women less privileged than you. But if you merely use your pen to write about how overwhelmed you were to see the sufferings of girls and blame Plan for working for change in this extremely challenging culture for girls and women, then you will be blocking positive change for the very girls you want to help.

Real change will come, not by merely providing schools, water, clinics and drugs, but when, as President Obama says, Africa (Nepal too) has strong institutions, including strong government which as the major duty bearer will use its resources to implement the rights of its citizens. And this is the change that Plan works for. This change, fundamental, sustainable and enduring, takes a long time.

Remittances

IRVINE WELSH

Irvine Welsh is the author of nine previous works of fiction, most recently *Reheated Cabbage*. He lives in Dublin.

1

On this transatlantic flight from Spain, bile is keening in my guts as I await my arrival in my homeland with a mix of excitement and dread. I am returning to the Dominican Republic after an absence of almost eight years, bearing distressing news of my younger sister, Renata, with whom I had a chance and disturbing encounter in Madrid.

Now it was my duty to convey news of this awful confrontation to my mother, Christina, and to see my Grandmother Aida, as well as meet for the very first time two young half-brothers and nephew.

Mami and I had never enjoyed a good relationship. Christina Mary Rodriguez was a country girl from Cocoseco, a small *campo* in the impoverished south of the country. Cocoseco was the sort of place where girls will take up and have a child with the first motorcycle-riding, card-playing, beer-drinking *mujeriego* that comes their way. Then he will either leave them, or worse, stay and simply become another child to look after. The girl might, usually with his blessing, dump the kid with her mother and go to work in one of the tourist hotels in the east, or become a *viajera* in Europe, usually Spain.

Christina was liberated – albeit briefly – from such a fate by the amorous intervention of my urbane and educated father. Jose Santos, a civil engineer from Santo Domingo, was overseeing the construction of the bridge over the Rio Negra as it runs past Cocoseco. The river, like many of the locals, had been displaced by hurricane damage which caused it to burst its banks and re-route itself. Rather than set it back on its old path, the authorities had decided that it was better off where it was, calling in my father to make its new course permanent by shoring up its banks and building a bridge to reconnect Cocoseco with the road to the city of San Juan.

My father was a man of twenty-eight years, from a 'good' (translated as wealthy) family, who had studied his chosen profession in America. Despite his schooling, he was still very much a Dominican male, and deferred gratification in matters sexual was not his forte. When he saw the honey-skinned, lithe-limbed Christina with her dark, bewitching eyes walking home from school, Jose was instantly smitten. He moved to talk to her in the way of Dominican men, where a conversation can be practically indistinguishable from a seduction. Still only fifteen, Christina was green enough to be flattered by the attentions of this educated man, a supervisor of what was regarded in the *campo* as a work of great progress. I, Elena Rosa Rodriguez, was the product of their congress.

Though Christina's fallen condition was a far from a rare occurrence in Cocoseco, young girls in our region were usually impregnated by local men, not sophisticated strangers from our capital city. Christina's mother, my grandmother, Mama Aida Rodriguez, was nonetheless bitterly disappointed. But my father was nothing if not a man of honour. He decided that Christina – and their baby – would live with him back in Santo Domingo in a *union libre* until she was old enough to formally marry him. Mama Aida relented in her opposition when it became clear that a payment would be made to her from my father's family.

I recall my Papi Jose as a warm and affectionate man, and I would like to think that there was a genuine love between him and the headstrong young Christina, at least at the start of their relationship. Jose found a small, comfortable house with a garden, near the centre of the city, and my mother gave birth to me. Despite the initial appeal of urban life and the challenge of motherhood, Christina soon found that she was isolated in Santo Domingo. She had no mother, grandmother or sisters around her to share the burden of childcare, and Jose's family had little interest in assisting her on a day-to-day basis. It would be fair to say that they, and in particular his mother, my other grandmother, Mama

Monica Santos, a poker-faced matriarch, believed Jose had fallen into circumstances beneath him, taking on a *campesino* and her child. Jose was absent too – his work with the transport authority frequently took him on many civil engineering projects outside of Santo Domingo, particularly to the east of the country, where the infrastructure for tourism was being developed.

As a child I have strong recollections of enjoying the days and weeks when Papi came home, only to cry in sorrow when he left us for his work. I commenced school at six, which I loved and was good at, making many friends. Just shortly before this, my sister, Renata Elisabeth, had arrived. What ought to have been a happy event proved a crushing blow for my mother. Christina could no longer cope with her loneliness in the city, and a couple of years later, she announced to my father that she was heading back out to Cocoseco with baby Renata and me. I was so unhappy and confused, as I was settled at my school and loved our life in Santo Domingo.

I cannot truly say how Jose responded to this news. I would hope his reaction was one of despair, and that he tried hard to convince her to stay. Yet honesty compels me to record that his relationship with Christina had severely deteriorated, and I was aware of the blazing rows between them. Later, Mami would claim that he had another woman in the east. I was certainly seeing less and less of him. When he did come home, he would take me to the cinema or a museum, then on to a seaside cafe to eat ice cream. 'I don't want to go to the south, Papi,' I would whine.

He would silence me with his jokes and tickling, and say that if I were ever unhappy in Cocoseco or anywhere else, he would come and take me away. Besides, because of his work he would probably see more of me there than he did in the capital. This invariably appeased me as I loved him and never doubted his word.

Mami finally made good her threat to move us to Cocoseco, and I hated it with a vengeance. It sat in a beautiful lush valley, all those magnificent shades of emerald vibrant under a haze of a golden sun which poured down from the almost cloudless blue skies above. A mountain range towered overhead and the air was cool and sweet after the city. Yet this uplifting impression was instantly shattered when we came into the town itself and I felt myself sinking into despair though Mami pumped my hand with glee. It was a settlement of grubby old clay shacks with rusting tin roofs. Barefoot feral children were running around in squalor, along with untethered animals: pigs, goats, *perros*, hens and ducks. Scrawny evil-looking *gatos* lurked in the shadows. Groups of youthful men stood on the corners, fixing motorcycles, hanging around corner bars, drinking beer, playing cards and listening to loud *bachata* music.

Our house was an old broken-down hovel with a ruinous roof which leaked when it rained. Inside it was partitioned with sheets which hung pinned to the rickety overhead wooden beams holding up the creaking roof. My bed was an itchy wooden cot I shared with Renata, in which I sweated and twisted, as mosquitoes grew plump on my blood while the noise of motorcycle engines, music and laughter kept me awake into the small hours. When I drifted into a sick sleep, the shrill belligerent crows of the neighbour's rooster would tear me into a flaky dawn consciousness. Worst of all, though, was the dirty floor of impacted earth covered by rough straw mats under my poor feet. Renata took to all this easily, she knew little else, but never a day went by that I did not pine for the luxury of our old house in Santo Domingo, with its water, electricity and toilet, and the city's concrete pavements and tarmac roads.

In Cocoseco, there was one dwelling that stood out from the others in its affluence, and we had the misfortune to be situated right across the street from it, its proximity underscoring our penury. 'This, of course, is all temporary,' Christina would boast, 'Papi is building a new house for us soon.' I could not wait. I looked across to what we called 'the good house', owned by Freda Sanchez, a well-dressed, imperious woman whom Christina detested.

'Will it be as good as Madame Sanchez's house, Mami?'

'Much, much better!' she would snap as Freda sat on her porch, wearing a superior, self-satisfied expression. 'Look at her, you know where the money comes from that she rubs in our faces,' Mami would bark so that she would be heard across the street, '*Ella es una quita marido!*'

Freda reciprocated this antipathy, and sometimes they would exchange bitter insults across the street. '*Hija de puta!*' she would shout at Christina.

'*Mama guevo!*' was Mami's inevitable reply.

Mami's ally in this constant duel was Maria Sosa, who lived next to us with her seven children. They would sit outside, numerous kids at their feet, making up stories about Freda and laughing like hyenas in response to their own wit.

Then, shortly after our departure to Cocoseco, we received news of a terrible event, which was to change our lives for ever. Papi was killed at work. Some say it was a freak accident, while others cited negligent and unsafe work practices. What is certain is that a bulldozer was building up the banking on the side of a road, following a storm which had caused the highway to subside. The machinery toppled over and crushed both Jose Santos and another civil engineer, Ramon Fernandez. My father was killed outright, while Ramon survived but required both his legs to be amputated. The driver of the tractor was unharmed. It was the bleakest day of my life: I truly felt as if I had lost everything. Seen through our grief, the smugness on the face of Freda Sanchez seemed more insulting than ever.

2

The weeks following my father's death were bleak, but then I was to receive some unexpectedly heartening news. The early scholastic promise I had shown had not been lost on Papi, whom, I discovered in delight, had left a trust fund for my education. This was to be posthumously administered by his family, which meant Mama Santos. However, in only two years between her birth and my mother's defection back to Cocoseco, he had neglected to set up any similar provision for Renata.

It was the news I'd needed to lift me from my debilitating gloom, having previously felt that I would be entombed in this place for ever. I had always tried to study hard, and I maintained a deep loathing for days when I was not in school. However, it was difficult to keep my focus. There was nothing in Cocoseco, or even in the closest city, San Juan, that came anywhere near to the amusements we had in Santo Domingo, with its cinemas, theatres, galleries and libraries which I had loved to visit with Papi. When everyone else is having fun, it is not easy to be a scholar. While other girls were thinking about boys, I daydreamed of a library, a place where you could sit all day in divine silence, surrounded by books. But at home there was nothing to do except hang around until Christina chased me from the house into the chaos outside, pronouncing me as abnormal when I got lost in the wonder of a book, usually given to me by my teacher Mina Gomez.

The school in Cocoseco was regarded as one of the best in the region, but to my mind it was primitive and tatty compared to what I had been used to. The students and staff were less motivated and did not attend regularly, though Mina Gomez was a great encouragement to me. Despite her help, I still might have given up, were it not for an extraordinary letter that I learned had been left to me by my father along with the trust fund details. The instructions were to pass it on to me when I graduated from the school, but as my father had died, Mama Santos and her lawyers thought I should receive it immediately.

My dearest Elena Rosa,

Please believe that my love for you has no boundaries and that you will always be my Princess. Endeavour, always, to remember that education and learning are your friends and that books are your allies in this great journey of life.

Do not think of Jesus as your friend, and please never believe that having a baby when you are still a child yourself can ever redeem a girl such as you. Do not think that a life of struggle in order to feed the many mouths you might be inclined to bring into this world is a virtue that will sanctify you. It is not and it will not. And please, never ever think of yourself as some sort of insurance policy for either of your parents.

Be strong and proud, and go and live your life on your own terms.

Yours always,

Papi

This letter inspired me, but it caused me much sadness, as I took its existence to mean that Papi had been intending to go far away, perhaps back to the USA. It also presented me with a big problem as I had to keep it hidden from Mami. Had Christina known of it, she would almost certainly have destroyed it out of rage and jealousy. She had received nothing from Jose or his family, and her plans for a dream house were gone for ever. We were condemned to live in the horrible shack.

I buried the letter in a spot by the river, close to what I called Papi's bridge, enclosing it in a red plastic bag to protect it from the rains. Although every line of it was stored in my head, I needed it as a keepsake. Sometimes my mind would play tricks on me and I'd ask myself, did he really say that? and I'd be compelled to go and dig it up to re-examine its contents for affirmation, before re-consigning it to the earth. I guarded my trips to the riverbank jealously – there was no such thing as privacy in Cocoseco.

While I sobbed most nights, Mami had never shown any real sorrow about Papi's terrible fate. But one day, when I was coming home from school, I saw her standing on the bridge he had built, looking down at the river he had re-routed. I swear there were tears in her eyes. I went to her and hugged her, but she pushed me away, and it was never mentioned again. I suppose she had other things to occupy her with Renata and myself. My sister meanwhile had scant recollection of her father, and had little to remember him by. Unlike me, she thrived in the *campo*.

Although I now looked forward to my goal of university, my existence grew more torturous with every passing day. I seemed to sprout breasts overnight, and every time I ventured outside the boys wouldn't leave me alone. I grew fearful and depressed by their gestures and remarks: I knew that only fraudulent intent lay behind their idiot grins and trickster words. I didn't want to sleep with any of them and I certainly didn't want a baby, unlike so many other girls. But then I learned to be clever: I pretended to be religious. I walked around with a distracted saintly air, and slept with a plastic figure of Jesus by my bed. This made me a favourite of Mama Aida, who pronounced me a girl of great virtue and grace. I loved my grandmother, but there was something slightly deranged about her. Sometimes when I went into the house, I would find her sitting alone in the dark, muttering like a lunatic in a thick country dialect I could barely understand.

3

Renata was Mami's favourite. She was always full of fun, an exuberant and playful young girl who was continually berating me for only being interested in my studies. Though we were close, we were very different in our outlook and sometimes fought. The one thing we did have in common was that we had both inherited Mami's temper and her obstinate nature. I was often supposed to be responsible for Renata when we were outside, but sometimes my younger sister would run away out of devilment. This always got me into trouble with Mami. 'You must take care of your sister!'

When she got to ten or eleven years old, our paths started to divert. The extreme flattery Renata received from older boys was much more than I ever had to endure. She was different; though at first she was as embarrassed as me, Renata soon started to look back and cock her head, enjoying her power over the boys, loving to illicit more nonsense from their mouths. She was cut from the same cloth as my mother.

Christina was constantly being wooed by the well-dressed *papichulo* of our village who went by the name of Benjamin. He always wore new shirts and expensive sunglasses, and drove the coolest, finest blue *motorconco* that anyone had seen. He also had the first cell phone in the *campo*. Once he volunteered to drive me into San Juan, so that I could visit the library there. I refused this offer; I was scared of Benjamin and avoided him. His hungry eyes seemed to follow you everywhere. Christina disdained him, while casually and light-heartedly spurning his attentions. 'He is so ugly. That one is wasting his time around here.'

I was growing more self-conscious; painfully aware of my difference from the other girls my age in Cocoseco, most of whom now had children. I carried myself badly, and was always getting told off or slapped around the head by Mami or Mama Aida for slouching when I walked, or for not looking at people. Mami had the harshest tongue but my grandmother was worse; from the shadows those heavy, bony knuckles would shoot out and rap your skull with the warning, 'Lift your head and keep your eyes off the ground!'

I did not eat well and food became a comfort to me. I guzzled as many sugar-laden fruit drinks as I could, and started to bloat. Renata, meantime, had entered an early puberty and had the figure of a slim but curvy film star. I would cross myself in public when there were groups of boys passing. Soon they started to ignore me, or more accurately the compliments stopped and became jokes.

Not quite all the boys acted that way. There was one, Rudy, who was my friend at school. He was a shy but studious boy, with a stammer that became pronounced when he grew nervous. The other boys mercilessly tormented him. They mocked his condition, and called him a *paricon* or a *palomo*. At school Rudy and I put on a play about a girl who slept with a boy who was pestering her to prove her love for him. The boy gave her AIDS. Her mother found out and killed the boy by stabbing him in the heat of the moment. That play was our revenge on Cocoseco. My friendship with Rudy served another handy purpose; everyone assumed that we were having sex, and left us both alone. This, when all we would do is just talk about theatre! He became my closest ally, and I even showed him Papi's letter.

I wanted to study drama properly, and dreamed of becoming an actress. The cinema in San Juan was only very occasionally operational, but films could be shown in Cocoseco on black market DVDs. Our neighbours, the

Sosa family, had a DVD player provided by Maria's absent husband, and the movies were my other main source of joy besides books. I would watch them with Mami, Renata and the Sosa girls, enthralled by the way they took me into all those different worlds.

*

Graduating from school was the best day of my life. I had my picture taken with my certificate, but Mami put it in the old trunk she kept by her bed. I took a bus to Santo Domingo to meet my grandmother Monica Santos, to discuss my future education. By now my dream was to study drama in New York City. Unfortunately, Mama Santos, who controlled the money and therefore the conditions of my trust fund, had decided that I would study Hotel and Catering Management at a university in North Carolina, USA, in the town of Chapel Hill. This way, she explained, I would be able to return to the Dominican Republic and work in the tourist industry. My father's people were patriots; his own father (and Mama Santos's husband) had been murdered for opposing the dictatorship of Trujilla. Mama Santos fervently believed that educated Dominicans had a duty to stay in the country and help to make it better. I sensed that was a viewpoint she had enforced upon my father.

But this was not what I wanted. It was my passionate desire to get away from the Dominican Republic and never return. I'd always had dreams of a different life, and only took proper interest in my family or neighbours when someone in the *campo* talked of a relative or a friend who had gone to live in New York or Spain. But while the course of study was not what I desired, North Carolina was the first step to a new life and I was excited to go.

4

I took little with me to the USA; in my haste to get away even my father's treasured note was left buried in its safe place. There would be time to retrieve it later, and I fantasised about briefly returning to Cocoseco as a success, and digging up the letter and reading it to Mami, before heading back to America for good.

In the event, it took longer that I thought to settle into Chapel Hill's student life. The campus at North Carolina was a different world; I came across few Dominicans and Latins in general seemed thin on the ground. But I loved the freedom, and as my English grew better, I made several friendships. Best of all was the study bedroom I had in the student apartment block on campus; everything was so fresh, with cleaners coming in to service it, and no chores, all we had to do was study! And of course, there was the amazing library. Without discussing it with Grandmother Santos, I changed my classes from Hotel and Catering Management to the more generic Business Studies, specialising in Marketing. In the interests of employment, I was prepared to forget about my dreams of becoming an actress. There was a drama society at the university which I joined, though self-conscious of my ever-increasing size (American food and its generous portions were irresistible after the DR), I kept behind the scenes, working in stage management.

I received regular news from Cocoseco, usually emails from Renata, who got ferried regularly to the Internet Café at San Juan by some boy on the back of his *motoconcho*. Her emails comprised mainly of gossip about the neighbours and boys, and the goings-on in the *campo*. This was much easier for me to engage with from my laptop in the luxury of my study bedroom on the North Campus Community at Chapel Hill. Then, suddenly, the correspondence stopped. As weeks and then months went by, I was forced to call Benjamin; Renata had sent his cell phone number in case of an emergency, and he informed me that my sister had been gone for almost six months. He then put me on to my mother who explained that Renata, just thirteen, had married, as she put it, a boy from a neighbouring *campo* and was having his child. The boy in question was 'no good' and Christina called Renata foolish, but still did not advise against her moving in with his mother and sisters. 'I have enough on my hands,' she said, informing me that she was soon to be a mother again.

I greeted the news with silence.

'Did you hear me?' she growled through the static.

'Who is to be the father?' I asked, and was not in the least surprised when she told me it was Benjamin.

'He has changed,' she contended. 'He now plans to go to university to study law and business.'

I wanted to tell her that she was delusional, that Benjamin studied nothing but the spots on dominoes and the curves of passing women, and never would, but this was unnecessary as it was evident that my silence had spoken in my stead.

It was sufficient to precipitate an attack on me. 'You think you can judge us all, with your education and your travelling! You'll be a cranky, virgin spinster like your po-faced grandmother Santos!'

I forget my reply, but it was something along the lines that, whatever else could be said about her, my father's mother could scarcely be described as a virgin. Logic was never Christina's strong point, however, and I learned that my religious charade had been convincing enough for her to be completely taken in by it, as she began to disparage my supposed service to God and Jesus.

I felt it was time to put her straight on that issue. 'I never cared about religion,' I cut in when she stopped for breath, 'I only pretended to do so to be left alone by the idiots in our shit-hole of a town, as I planned my escape from the festering squalor of your home. The figure of Christ I only used to pleasure myself with,' I hissed.

This was a lie, but it stopped Christina in her tracks. I heard her gasp; it was as if that figurine had just breached her in the very way that I had described. '*Cuero!*' She shouted through the static, as prayers spilled from her mouth into my ear for the first time ever, asking God and his son to forgive me. How much was in response to Mami's genuine shock and how much in her customary habit of guilt-tripping was impossible to ascertain.

5

I was deeply concerned about Renata's fate, and checked my email regularly, but still no contact was forthcoming. Each time I called Christina we ended up arguing, but I sensed that she was growing tired. My mother now had a son, and she told me that there was another baby on the way. Benjamin was in hospital, he had got into a fight with a man at the *gallera* – inevitably over money or women – and his lung was punctured by a knife. It seemed to me appropriate that he was injured at the *pelea de gallos*, and I felt no remorse at all. Christina herself seemed to care little; she sent him back to his mother's to be nursed (or Benjamin had simply gone there, I never got the real story) while she bore and raised their second son.

It was after the arrival of this child that Mami started exhorting me to abandon my studies and return to the DR. 'I need you to come back and help me!' she wailed. 'I have two sons, your baby brothers! And your nephew, little Luis, your only sister's child; you have never even seen them! Come back and help me!'

In spite of everything, and as much as I loved my studies and my life in Chapel Hill, I was prepared to give them up and go back to Cocoseco and do my duty. But then I thought about how hard I had worked and remembered my father's words in that letter buried in the soft, rich soil by the banks of the Rio Negra.

... never ever think of yourself as some sort of insurance policy for either of your parents.

When I think back to this time, it scares me how close I was to throwing it all away, and going back to a place that I hated, subsidising a lifestyle I deplored, and for someone I had grown to have such contempt for. So I stayed on. But still the calls came, no matter how expensive they must have been from Benjamin's cell phone, of which Christina now seemed to have permanent possession. Never was Renata's name volunteered, and when I asked Mami about my sister's life in her new home, she was evasive or spoke in generalities. Yet she continued to plead with me for help. There was always something. One of the boys had a fever: a charity was helping with medicines, but she needed her daughter here. A storm had damaged our home and ruined our meagre possessions: in such trying circumstances, the help of her daughter was essential. Two members of a family in the *campo* had drowned, trying to get to Puerto Rico. I had to come back.

Why, I thought, why? What can I do? 'Go and get Renata to help! She is your favourite!' I shouted.

It was then Mami confessed to me that Renata had vanished from her mother-in-law's home in San Marco, the neighbouring town to Cocoseco. At fifteen years of age she had simply walked out one day, leaving her new family, apparently bound for New York with a friend. Renata had left her infant son at her sister-in-law's, but they had promptly dispatched him back to Christina and Grandmother Aida. Now Christina had three small boys to look after, her own pair (one and two years old) and their two-year old nephew!

At that point, rather than buckle, I became strangely fortified. Through the lens of my student life in the United States, I resolved that I was never going back to that place of madness, there was no way a modern woman could live such an existence. To my mind, the women that did live back in Cocoseco were now practically indistinguishable from the multi-teated black *puercos*, goats and bitch-dogs that were tethered miserably in the compacted yards by the tin-roofed shacks, left to rake through piles of festering garbage for old morsels.

Mami did not take this well, particularly when I was moved to verbalise my reservations, and she deployed some of the curses previous used on Freda Sanchez. '*Asarosa! Puta!*'

Her scorn meant little, however, and her concerns were at best peripheral to the life I was leading on the college campus. I had finally found a boyfriend, Eric, a sincere Colombian engineering student. We were thrown together by the prejudices of race and size which decreed that as the two overweight Latins on campus (to say nothing of being desperate virgins) we were meant to be together. So we became a couple; two fat and studious nerds who explored each other's flabby bodies with fevered lust, excited and repelled in almost equal measure by what we discovered.

I learned that there is nothing like getting fucked to change one's perspective on life. Things that seem crucial and lead to prudishness or obsession tend to pale into insignificance in the face of the power of sexual gratification. I looked at the people whom I had scorned back home in a somewhat different light. I realised that the problem with places like

Cocoseco was not their culture of promiscuity, just the fact that this went in tandem with a lack of individual responsibility and the absence of women's rights. It thus helped to keep women oppressed and men in a permanent state of infantilism. Again, it was my books, and in this case feminist writings, which provided me with the tools to understand who I was and where I had come from.

Eric and myself made a pact to get in shape, changing our diets and visiting the campus gym regularly. I found it easier to stay on course (poor Eric never managed to kick his addiction to American food: candy, Coca-Cola, hot dogs, burgers and fries), and the pounds started flying off, to the point that other men were soon noticing me. To Eric's sadness, one was Alexi; a Ukrainian, who was a passionate, powerhouse lover. I suppose that it was this *gringo* who further helped me find the Dominican woman within me, the one I had forcibly repressed for so long.

6

A fuller life did not curtail my focus on my studies and I graduated second-from-top in my year, with an excellent degree. Crucially, this enabled me to obtain a bursary to go on to New York City and take a master's qualification, and I now no longer had financial dependence on Mama Santos. New York suited me even better than Chapel Hill, as there were many Dominicans in the city and I moved into the community at Washington Heights, sharing an apartment close to Juan Pablo Duarte Boulevard. I loved the Spanish-speaking life on the asphalt of 163rd Street, and on the sidewalks of bustling St Nicholas Boulevard. At times it felt as if all of Santo Domingo was here, with the Dominican flag flying proudly from balconies, apartment windows, storefronts and *patelito* stands. Following his graduation, Alexi went back to Kiev, and our relationship fizzled out in cyberspace over a string of emails.

I met my next boyfriend, Victor, at a local theatre group's comedy improv production. He was a second-generation Dominican but had only been to the old country once. Nonetheless, he had a rose-tinted fascination for it, and hated me deriding the place. 'You'll be estranged from yourself as long as you're alienated from where you grew up. The Westerners feel that they want to condemn our poverty, because it affronts them. Well, I want to condemn their misery. It affronts me! Let them do something about that first; fix their own miserable, unhappy lives!'

Victor could afford that perspective. His parents were socialists who had fled the Trujillo regime and had made money in the USA. He wanted for nothing, and had just finished a film studies degree at NYU. As cynical as I was, however, I had to concede that there was some truth in what he said. Looking back on my childhood, I saw the misery I remembered was all mine, and mine alone, and spread by me to others in the form of my constant city-girl's grumblings about life in Cocoseco. In retrospect, I had been a beacon of gloom. Renata, and even Christina in her own way, resembled the other villagers; in spite of their squabbles they were essentially happy souls.

In New York, and America in general, in spite of (or perhaps because of) the material wealth, people often seemed so joyless and depressed. A commonplace incident brought this home to me. One day, on the subway, I was crushed next to a man reading a novel, smelling of beer and cigarettes, his pores secreting slow-mo bullets of sweat before my very eyes. His shoulder, hip and leg were welded to mine, and I could feel our breathing synchronise. I noticed suddenly that there were tears in his eyes, and as I only saw this man in profile, I would never know what this book had said to him or had triggered in him, that moved him so. I wanted to ask, but by the time I was emboldened he had risen and was gone. I thought about the madness of those transitory intimacies which doomed us to know nothing of each other, and for the first time, I yearned for home. I thought of Rudy, Christina, Mama Aida, those children I had never seen, and even Grandmother Monica Santos back in

Santo Domingo. But most of all, I longed to speak to Renata.

She was supposed to be somewhere in this great city, working in a restaurant, but still there was no response to my emails and Christina would not divulge her whereabouts, if indeed she knew them. I asked around Washington Heights; nobody had seen her. Almost every time I passed a restaurant I was compelled to look inside. My phone calls to Mami invariably ended on her usual note of complaint: 'Both my daughters have abandoned me! What selfish children I have raised!'

On graduating for the second time with a master's degree in Applied Marketing, I took a job as a lecturer in a community college in Long Island. It was decent pay and for the first time I was able to send money back home to Mami. I would go to my local Western Union office every fortnight after I was paid my salary, and send whatever *remesa* I could afford on to her. This had the immediate effect of quelling her histrionics on the phone and made her less inclined to suggest that I should give up my life here and return to the Dominican Republic.

In time though, my old relationship with Christina began to reassert itself. Soon the money I sent was never enough. She would call me a *tacano*, and worse, while I referred to her as a dirty *campesino*, fearing that my hard-earned cash was being squandered on shirts for Benjamin, or some other idler that she'd taken up with. Every time I sent her payments, in my mind's eye I could see Christina inside the Vimenca in San Juan, counting out the pesos, a taut sneer of entitlement pulling at her features.

I enjoyed working in Long Island, although it was further from the city than I would have liked. The trek was arduous, involving the subway ride from 168th and Broadway to Penn Station and then an MTA commuter train to the college. I got on well with my students, but after a while, I decided I wanted to move on and applied for a similar post in Spain. I had broken up with Victor. It was yet another sad ending, as with Alexi and Eric, but like them, I felt blessed by knowing him. Victor and I were unable to keep our hands off each other, but this papered over the cracks of two fundamentally incompatible sorts; I was a doer and he was a dreamer. All he talked of were his ideas for screenplays I knew would never be written, and films that would never be made. A new business partner, usually a producer or financer, would be put on a pedestal, only for the relationship to subsequently dissolve in bitter recrimination with unreturned phone calls. Our fights were as tempestuous as our love-making, and something had to give. Spain seemed to offer a change of scene and a new adventure.

7

I flew to Madrid to attend the interview. I was staying with Mariasela, a New York Dominican friend who had earlier relocated to that city. I took some summer leave during the college recess, planning to stay in Europe for three weeks. At the interview, the Spanish spoken sounded so formal and elegant that I felt more like an ignorant peasant speaking in my own tongue than I ever did talking English in America.

There were many Dominicans in Spain, the vast majority of them women. Mariasela's boyfriend, Severiano, was a Spaniard, and he joked about the supposed sexual insatiability of Dominican girls. I did not take too kindly to this as I had known only three boyfriends, and had led a far from promiscuous life. I have a temper, and I was somewhat on edge after the interview, so I carried the argument on that night as we went to a bar. I grew increasingly annoyed with Mariasela; she seemed to be taking Severiano's part, against her own countrywomen. While she said nothing in essence that I did not agree with, and she was inoffensive when compared to Severiano's increasingly hostile taunts, I did not think it appropriate to focus only on the negative side of our society in front of foreigners. At North Carolina and New York, I would always stress the good things about my country: its intense natural beauty and the generosity and laughter of its people.

Suddenly Severiano looked out the big window and pointed across the street to two very young women who were going into an apartment block. He said in his teasing leer, 'They are Dominican prostitutes who work from an apartment run by an escort agency. They take their tricks there!'

I was not concerned with his words, because all I could see was that one of them was my sister Renata! Here, in Madrid.

The fury and frustration welled in me and I rose and threw my rum-and-cola drink into Severiano's face. It trickled down onto his silk shirt and his white jacket. He screamed abuse at me, shouting at the waiter to furnish him with a cloth. As he ranted, all I saw was the spoiled face of privilege. Later, I would speculate; was that the same emotion my mother grew to feel when she looked at my father? Had his affectations and those of his family really become so repulsive to her? Was it the humiliation of their rejection that compelled her to leave Santo Domingo for Cocoseco?

We all went home, still quarrelling, Mariasela in tears, and I took my belongings and left their apartment, checking into a modest hotel. Mariasela (and, I must admit, even Severiano) protested, trying to salvage our friendship as she implored me to at least stay the night and think it over once we had calmed down. But my own temper and the cruellest coincidence had soured everything, and I needed to be alone so that I could confront Renata without outsiders knowing of our family disgrace.

8

The next day I went back to the same bar, took the identical seat in the window that faced out onto the apartment, and waited. After less than an hour I saw Renata come back with a man, an old business type who wore fine clothes. He left about thirty minutes later. Then another man came to the apartment. I could see the lights go on and off. Then another. I went out onto the street to get a closer look at the comings and goings. I once saw Renata stare out the window, before an old *gringo* put his arms around her and pulled her back into the room. I was cold and there were all sorts of undesirables hanging around. One slimy creep with gold teeth and greasy hair looked at me and made a lewd proposition.

'*Mama guevo! Hijo de puta!*' I cursed at him.

The smile never left his face. I moved away and rang the bell to Renata's apartment and was buzzed in without having to speak on the intercom.

To my surprise, the door in the apartment I judged to be hers was ajar. Inside it was sweet smelling and softly lit. Renata had evidently been expecting someone: no doubt another client. I could hear her disembodied voice, coming from the bathroom. 'You're early tonight, you bad boy. I'm just getting myself ready for you. You are so naughty, coming early and trying to catch me unawares like this!'

My heart sank at her words. It was true, she was more than just a *viajera*; she was a *cuero*.

Wearing a black negligee, and taking a swig from a bottle of Volvic, Renata stepped into the room. She was as slender as ever, and still looked like the teenager she was, but something had hardened in her eyes. She was shocked into silence when she saw me standing beside the white leather couch, no doubt looking chaste with my handbag in front of me.

Her eyes narrowed on me, 'Who the fuck are you and what are you doing here? If you think you're working this apartment you can think again. Call Geraldo at the agency and you'll find out that we're booked in here . . .'

I never expected that she would fail to recognise me. But it had been seven years, eighty pounds and several dress sizes. I smiled at her. 'You sound so like Mami!'

Her face expanded in recognition. 'Elena! My God! I don't believe it!'

'Hi, Sis,' I said, but as I advanced towards her, I saw

that distraction and calculation had already entered her mind, and I received only a tense, perfunctory hug.

'You have to go.'

'No way, we need to catch up, the emails I sent . . .'

'I'm expecting company. You really must go. Now!'

'Look,' I averted my eyes from her briefly to let them stray around the apartment, taking in its sleek, minimalist furnishings; a brown leather settee, glass coffee table, plasma television set and a generously filled cocktail cabinet. 'I know what you're doing here.'

'You know nothing,' she spat with ferocity. 'Just get out of here!'

'Renata . . . it's been so long . . . we have to catch up . . .'

'There's nothing to catch up with! Go! Get out of my sight!' She pointed to the door.

I didn't know what to say. I knew that my mother had deep grievances against me, but I never imagined that Renata felt the same. 'Why are you rejecting me like this?'

'What the fuck are you talking about? Me rejecting *you*, the trust fund girl!'

'I only left in order to better myself . . .' I faltered. She had never had that opportunity, and I was now realising just what that meant to her.

'The letter,' she smiled cruelly. I swear my heart fell into my stomach.

There was nothing I could say.

'Your silly little letter. The one Papi left you. The one you buried.'

'How . . . how do you know? . . .'

'It's gone. I burned it.'

I fought my anger down, trying to remember my drama training. Keep thinking in the abstract. It was only a piece of paper. What mattered were the sentiments contained in it, and these will stay with me until I die. 'It doesn't matter,' I said sadly. 'How did you find it?'

'Remember your Rudy, with the stammer?'

Rudy. I wanted to say that he was never mine, or at least not in the way she thought, but I resolved to keep my silence.

'He missed you when you left and started hanging around me when I came back to Cocoseco to visit Mami. He kept asking me for news of you. We chatted and he let slip about the letter. He wouldn't tell me where it was at first,' she smiled, briefly a teasing little girl again, 'but I managed to persuade him.'

'Renata, it doesn't matter . . .'

'Correct. It doesn't matter at all. Now get the fuck out of here and go back to New York or North Carolina or wherever. Just because you've lost some weight and learned how to put on make-up, it doesn't make you any less of a stuck-up frigid lesbian bitch. Now fuck off!'

I was shaken and physically trembling. I had been

totally unprepared for this rejection and her spiteful whorish vitriol.

Just as I made to depart, a tall, middle-aged man with spiky but receding blond hair came in. He was well-dressed and spoke with a Dutch or German sounding accent.

'Aha . . . it is my lucky day, yes Angelina?'

I winced at the mention of Renata's whore name. I felt sick to my core at the notion of my sister giving her body to all those strangers.

'Two ladies for the price of one . . . but, it *will* be the price of one,' the visitor added emphatically.

'It's only me, Ronald. My friend is just leaving,' Renata looked hatefully at me.

'OK,' I conceded, beaten and cowed, feeling for the first time in years like the fat, stooping girl in Cocoseco, and now just wanting to be out of this nightmare and back into the sane life I had built for myself. 'You know my email if you want to get in touch,' I said meekly.

Renata remained silent, but her blazing eyes ushered my departure.

'It's a shame you are going,' the oily Dutchman or German purred as I exited.

The next day at the hotel, I rose miserably and after breakfast checked my emails. I learned through Mariasela that the college where I had been interviewed had got in touch, and I was to call them. A departmental secretary informed me that I was regrettably unsuccessful on this occasion. This no longer concerned me; I did not want to be in Madrid if my sister was here, earning her living in this vile way. My Spanish dream was now hopelessly tainted. I cursed her and the whores like her who had given Dominican women like myself a bad name in Spain; I even managed to blame her for my failure at the interview. All I thought about was my precious letter. It represented what I loved most about Cocoseco, and she had destroyed it through spite and jealousy.

I was able to change my flight tickets and was planning to head back to New York early. It was then I had the inspiration: I still had time left before returning to work and I would use it to go back home to the Dominican Republic. Mami needed to know about Renata.

9

Santo Domingo airport had changed for the better; it was tidier and more ostentatiously wealthy. I rented a car and drove into the city. As I sat in Panavi, a chic pastry café on Gustavo Mejia Ricart, I could have been somewhere fashionable in Madrid or NewYork City. It was evident that alongside the poverty, there was a growing sophisticated professional class, and I even toyed with the notion that there might be a place for me in my home country.

I had felt the obligation to visit my grandmother Santos although we had no relationship beyond that of the sponsored and the fund administrator. In her eyes, I was not the last remnant of her dead son, but rather the living evidence of the 'whore that had destroyed him'. Grand-mother Santos believed that my mother was some kind of jezebel, who, by getting together with my father, had determined that his fate would be a grizzly one. Then she'd sealed this by abandoning him, his subsequent grief making him careless, causing him to be under the path of that tumbling bulldozer. Sometimes this passive marital distraction was refined into something more sinister; a positive curse by this country witch. This led her to another obsession, with that of the Haitian construction workers whom my father supervised. They were also candidates for culpability in his demise, especially as one of them was driving the upturned bulldozer, and survived unharmed. 'Filthy African cannibal pigs,' she spat, 'let them stay in their own cesspit of a country!'

Some things never changed: no matter how bad circumstances were here, Haitians would always be worse off and the targets of our fear and loathing. Experience had taught me that every nation in the world seemed to need a detested neighbour as a scapegoat. Living in New York, I had learned that Puerto Ricans often entertained similar prejudices about us Dominicans.

I stayed one tense and desperate night at the home of this embittered woman before heading to what we call 'the south' (though, for the first time I realised, I was actually travelling west) in the modest car I'd rented at the airport. The road to Azua was teeming with workmen, just as it was when I left over seven years ago. I recall this as Papi had taken me out there. In this time the work seemed to have progressed little, though my mind might be playing tricks on me.

I made progress onto the San Juan road, the country as beautiful as I remembered it, and got to Cocoseco just as the light was beginning to fade. The town was also very much the same, or so I thought until I got to my mother's house. There I could scarcely believe the evidence of my eyes. The old clay and tin-roofed shack was gone, and instead, there was a stucco mock-colonial house with pillars, gate, railings, patio, with the walls painted a mustard colour. There was further evidence that it was a piecemeal development with construction work to the rear still very much ongoing. It had pride of place on this side of Cocoseco.

My head made a brief, involuntary turn across the road to Freda's home, and yes, our place was grander. As I looked back to confirm this, I noticed that my mother was sitting on the porch, with a woman who looked familiar and a man who sparked no recognition in me. They appeared very relaxed in their moulded white plastic chairs. Christina was fuller of face and body, and she wore a green tank top and side button-up jeans, which stopped at her calves. Her thighs had taken the biggest hit of fat; they looked meaty, encased in that tight denim. Her hair was pinned back and had been newly straightened, and she wore gold-hooped earrings. I suddenly recognised the smiling woman next to her. I could not believe that Freda Sanchez, Mami's formerly detested rival, was sitting with her on the porch drinking iced mango juice.

Mami smiled wanly at me but made no attempt to rise. Instead she simply said to the others, 'My daughter has returned. Look at her!' Then she turned to me, 'Do they not feed you in America?' And as she broke into a tight grin, I found myself fighting back tears that were welling in my eyes.

'Please excuse us, Freda,' Christina said, somewhat haughtily. 'Federico, bring the boys to see their sister and aunt, and tell her grandmother Aida that our Elena Rosa has finally graced us with her presence.'

I now almost had to stifle a laugh. It was as if Christina was playing a villain in a James Bond movie. It made me realise, for the first time, what a master of manipulating her emotions and those of others she was. My actress dreams may have perished, but it was Mami who had the real family talent in this direction.

Freda Sanchez rose and greeted me with a hug; she was still a graceful, bird-like woman. I could feel her small bones, and I smelt a pleasing fragrance on her. The man Federico came forward, slightly shyly, and extended his hand. 'It's good to meet you,' he said. It seemed that Christina had at last found a man who delighted in being dominated by her.

'You've done well, Mami,' I said, taking one of the seats, 'the house . . . it's beautiful.'

She accepted the compliment with a smug, affirmative nod, before a pang of melancholy burst in her. 'You know, your father once said he'd build me a big house here. It was all I ever wanted.'

'Then I'm glad the money I sent was of good use.'

Christina looked quizzically at me.

'In a sense Papi did pay for this big house,' I explained, with a growing sense of foreboding. 'After all, he bequeathed me the money to go to college, and with my academic job I was able to send you the money . . .'

Mami laughed and shook her head, brushing a fly from her face. 'Your money . . . it could not have paid for all this,' she said, her humor dissolving into tones low and pitying.

'What?'

'Renata. It was her *remesa* that paid for this. She sends me the money every week: as regular as clockwork. Lots and lots of money. Yes, Renata's money built this.' Christina ran her hands over one of the ornate railings in front of the window. 'She is a success,' she declared, turning away from me and raising her glass to her lips with a slight smile on her face.

I felt my blood starting to boil in my veins. I had intended to convey my grim news as diplomatically as possible. That urge had now left me. 'Do you know what she does to make her money?'

'She is children's nanny to a very wealthy family in New York City.'

'Nonsense!'

'It is the truth!'

'But I have seen her selling herself in Madrid, mother. *Ella estra cuereando en Espania!*'

My mother merely shrugged, as if acknowledging this terror was a minor concession, and looked at me with sunken eyes. She glanced around furtively before dropping her voice. 'If she'd stayed here she would just have given it away for nothing. Which is the greater crime?'

I felt deflated; I would never replace Renata in my mother's affections. 'Do you wish for me to keep sending the money?'

A big fake smile spread across Christina's face. 'Of course. It all helps. *El dinero de alli rinde aqui.* You are a good girl. A good girl to come home and see your old mother! Not like your sister, living *el vida alegra*.'

'It's good to see you, Mami,' I smiled weakly, taking her hands in my lap. It was the most intimate I can recall us being since I was an infant.

Christina whispered to me, 'You must say nothing of Renata to your Mama Aida: nor to Freda Sanchez. They think she is in New York, working hard in a restaurant.'

'Yes . . .' I couldn't help teasing, '. . . how strange that you're now such good friends with Freda!'

'She's a decent woman,' Christina said sincerely, and then looked tetchily next door, where children, black pigs and ducks ran around the same tin shack, and a sly, low-belly *viralata* skulked under the feet of Maria Sosa and her sister as they took in some washing, averting their eyes from Christina's harsh gaze. 'She is not the problem in this community!'

Federico came back like the pied piper, leading a large group of children. I could see Aida, hobbling behind them, trying to keep up. Christina gleefully pointed out three small boys from the crowd, and introduced them to me. 'Meet your brothers and nephew!'

Three pairs of ravenous eyes glared at me from the dusky twilight. One half-brother had a harelip and I saw him pinch a young girl with braided hair and a bite mark on her face. The other, a runny-nosed runt, climbed onto my lap, as if on cue. Luis, my father's grandson, interests me more. He stands back, and I can see Papi in him, his big sad eyes ensuring my donations will not stop. I'm not my parents' insurance policy, my father said, and he was right. But what about those mites, one of whom is his grandson, and who eerily has his look? What insurance will they have?

Mama Aida greeted me; lame from a collision she had with a youth who lost control of his *motoconcho*. I took more greetings then, exhausted from the travel, went inside to lie down in a proper room, on a bed which has been vacated by two of the boys. On the walls in the living room I had been shocked but moved to note framed pictures of me in various graduations; school, bachelors degree and master's. There were pictures of the children, and some of Renata, but mine took pride of place.

With cool tiles replacing the filthy mat-covered floors under my feet, I fell into bed and the best sleep I have ever had in Cocoseco.

10

Some things will never change: the crowing of the neighbour's rooster wakes me up. I lie in bed for a while, stretching out, luxuriating, drinking in my new surroundings.

When I get up and dress, I find that Mami has prepared scrambled eggs for breakfast. She now has a kitchen area with a proper *American* cooker, and the house has a generator. In the dining area, as well as the chairs and tables, there is a television set, DVD player, music system and many CDs. I cannot help but think about Renata, being used like a toilet by filthy strangers, in order that her family can enjoy those luxuries.

After breakfast I take a walk and find myself down by the river. I walk over Papi's bridge and look down on the slow, muddy Rio Negra trickling down towards its delta, and find it inconceivable that something so puny can wreak such havoc in the rainy season. I am close to the spot where I buried the letter, and my mind races back to that Madrid apartment and Renata's cruel boasts of her despicable deed. I am moved to investigate. When I remove the big stones and dig, I see some red plastic exposed. Inside the filthy, crumpled bag, I am astonished to find that the letter is still there! Renata did not destroy it. Instead, written as a footnote at the bottom of the page, in big, black capitals are the words:

I WAS HIS DAUGHTER TOO.

And so she was. The child Papi never had much time for, the one who was just an imposition on his busy life.

The girl of Cocoseco, who would lead a different life to the one from Santo Domingo.

I head into the car and drive to San Juan, spending the day looking around, and then sending emails back to friends in New York and to Mariasela in Madrid, with a heartfelt apology for my behaviour. As I send the last one away, a new correspondence jumps into my inbox. My heart almost stops, as I immediately see that it's from Renata.

Dearest Elena,

I beg you to please forgive my terrible behaviour yesterday. I was just so ashamed to be seen by you in the horrible and foul circumstances of what has become my life. I really would like to see you again, but not until I have stopped doing what I am doing.

I also want you to know that I did not destroy your letter, though I fear that in my anger I may have defaced it. Once again, please forgive me.

I have sent money back for Mami and for Ramon, Caesar and Luis. But I have kept some money back for myself and I am to marry a Dominican boy who has American citizenship. I hope to see you in New York City soon.

Yours in love,
Renata.

I write back immediately, and then she follows, and the communication floods between us for most of the day. Then she has to go back to what she does and, drained, I climb into the car and drive home to Cocoseco.

As the hot sun starts to drift towards the horizon, I see that they're all gathering around, filling the porch and front yard; producing bottles of Presidente. The men are complimenting me as only Dominican men can, welcoming me home. I'm ensnared in genuine love and affection, and my mother looks at me, then sobs, falling into her own mother's arms. And I have say that as much as I doubt I can stay here, with Papi's letter burning in the pocket of my jeans, part of me has been waiting for this moment all of my life. Now I have more letters; those precious emails between the scholar and the prostitute, documenting the remittances that can never be made good.